HEROES OF THE WOMEN'S SUFFRAGE MOVEMENT

SOJOURNER TRUTH

WOMEN'S RIGHTS ACTIVIST AND ABOLITIONIST

CATHERINE BERNARD

Enslow Publishing

101 W. 23rd Street
Suite 240
New York, NY 10011
USA

enslow.com

For my lovely, passionate, and awesome Matthew and my kind, creative, and amazing Evan.

Published in 2017 by Enslow Publishing, LLC.
101 W. 23rd Street, Suite 240, New York, NY 10011

Library of Congress Cataloging-in-Publication Data

Names: Bernard, Catherine.
Title: Sojourner Truth: women's rights activist and abolitionist / Catherine Bernard.
Description: New York : Enslow Publishing, 2017 | Series: Heroes of the women's suffrage movement |
Includes bibliographical references and index.
Identifiers: ISBN 9780766078871 (library bound)
Subjects: LCSH: Truth, Sojourner, 1799-1883—Juvenile literature. | African American abolitionists—
Biography—Juvenile literature. | Abolitionists—United States—Biography—Juvenile literature. | Social
reformers—United States—Biography—Juvenile literature. | African American women—Biography—
Juvenile literature.
Classification: LCC E185.97.T8 B44 2017 | DDC 306.3'62'092—dc23

Printed in the United States of America

To Our Readers: We have done our best to make sure all websites in this book were active and appropriate when we went to press. However, the author and the publisher have no control over and assume no liability for the material available on those websites or on any websites they may link to. Any comments or suggestions can be sent by e-mail to customerservice@enslow.com.

Portions of this book originally appeared in the book *Sojourner Truth: Abolitionist and Women's Rights Activist.*

Photo Credits: Cover, Hulton Archive/Getty Images; cover, interior design elements: wongwean/
Shutterstock.com (grunge background on introduction, back cover); Attitude/Shutterstock.com (purple
background); Sarunyu_foto/Shutterstock.com (white paper roll); Dragana Jokmanovic/Shutterstock.com
(gold background); Eky Studio/Shutterstock.com (grunge background with stripe pattern); macknimal/
Shutterstock.com (water color like cloud); Borders-Kmannn/Shutterstock.com (vintage decorative orna-
ment); p. 5 Time Life Pictures/Getty Images; p. 8 File:Sojourner truth c1870.jpg/Wikimedia Commons;
pp. 11, 13, 21, 31, 61, 71, 77, 87, 92, 99 Library of Congress; p. 17 File:1903 HardenberghHouseBk.
jpg/Wikimedia Commons; pp. 24–25 Leemage/Getty Images; p. 29 Universal History Archive/
UIG/Getty Images; pp. 33, 56, 58–59, 69, 83 Everett Historical/Shutterstock.com; pp. 36–37 File:
Microcosm of London Plate 064 - Quakers' Meeting (tone).jpg/Wikimedia Commons; pp. 41, pp. 44–45,
48 © North Wind Picture Archives; p. 64 File: Frederick Douglass by Samuel J Miller, 1847-52.png/
Wikimedia Commons; p. 89 MPI/Getty Images; p.103 MPI/Getty Images; p. 105 The White League
and the Ku Klux Klan: Worse than Slavery, cartoon from Harper's Weekly, 1874 (engraving) (b&w photo),
Nast, Thomas (1840-1902)/Private Collection/Bridgeman Images; p. 106 Jim West/Alamy Stock
Photo; p. 109 © AP Images.

CONTENTS

SOJOURNER TRUTH AND NINETEENTH CENTURY SOCIAL REFORM

❚❚ We hold these truths to be self-evident: that all men and women are created equal; that they are endowed by their Creator with certain inalienable rights; that among these are life, liberty, and the pursuit of happiness."[1]

At first glance, it seems easy to identify the source of these familiar sounding words. They must come from the Declaration of Independence, right? In fact, they are from an 1848 document titled The Declaration of Sentiments. They were written at a convention of women's rights advocates, convened more than 70 years after the original Declaration. The major change from one version to the other is the simple but powerful addition of the phrase "and women." Despite its lofty goals, the original Declaration of Independence essentially excluded the rights of women and minorities.

During the antebellum years, or the years before the U.S. Civil War, women were regularly denied the same rights as men. Many girls of

Since colonial times, women in America had few rights. They were considered the property of their husbands. They could not vote. And educational opportunities were rare.

this era did have the opportunity to attend some amount of public school but were discouraged from obtaining a higher education. The few white women privileged enough to attend college were limited to single-sex universities. In fact, by 1852 only two colleges in the country—Oberlin and Antioch College, both in Ohio—had co-educational enrollment. Career opportunities for graduates were limited largely to teaching or nursing. Most women were expected to become wives and mothers.

Nineteenth-century American women also lacked political and economic status. Married women or daughters who earned money from any profession made less money than their male counterparts. They weren't allowed to keep the money they earned. A married woman and her children were considered the legal property of her husband, as were any wages earned. In rare cases of divorce, women were not allowed to take custody of their children. Women were denied the right to vote or hold elected office.

While there were always equal rights advocates of any era, the women's rights movement as a whole gained real momentum in the early part of the nineteenth century. In large part the women's rights movement was influenced by another major social reform of the day—the campaign to end slavery, also known as abolitionism. For many, the push to end slavery was a moral and religious issue. As white Christian women began participating in the abolitionist cause, they were exposed to like-minded activists willing to challenge the status quo. Female abolitionists gained experience organizing, petitioning and even speaking publicly on behalf of basic human rights. The extension of their own rights as women was a natural progression of the abolitionist movement.

Many women's rights activists were indeed abolitionists, but few had direct experience in both spheres—that is, as a former slave and as a woman. One of the most powerful figures in each reform movement happened to be both. Former slave, Sojourner Truth, was proud to be a black woman fighting on behalf of the causes of both her race, and her gender. In fact, the speech Sojourner Truth is most well-known for remains, even today, one of the most powerful reminders of black feminism.

AIN'T I A WOMAN?

By the mid-nineteenth century, many women's rights advocates were inspired to organize local political events. These conventions provided opportunities to discuss important women's rights issues, such as educational reform, equal job opportunities, and the right to vote. In May 1851, a woman named Frances Gage gathered hundreds of people in Akron, Ohio for just such an event. On the afternoon of the second day, the crowd began to lose focus as hecklers were

After escaping to freedom, former slave Sojourner Truth devoted her life to the causes of abolitionism and women's rights. Truth famously delivered a stirring speech known as "Ain't I a Woman?" at an Akron, Ohio, women's convention in 1851.

disrupting the proceedings. That's when Sojourner Truth took the stage.

Speakers had been on all day, but many guests were surprised when Truth stepped on stage. The reason was very simple—Truth was the *only* black person at the convention. The color of her skin would not stop her from speaking, however, or from responding to the men disrupting the proceedings. The moment Truth began to speak, a hush fell over the crowd. No one could help but listen to her deep and powerful voice.[2]

Born a slave in New York in the late 1790s, Sojourner Truth never learned to read or write. As a result, almost all of what is known of her life comes from other people's accounts of her. The famous story of the Akron speech, for example, was related twelve years later by the president of the convention, Frances Gage. Truth knew what was being written about her, though. She was an extremely savvy woman who understood the importance of having her name widely known. For Truth, Gage's publication of her story simply meant more publicity for her cause.[3] In fact, Gage's version of the speech became so well-known that it is part of the foundation of Sojourner Truth's legend.

By 1851, Truth had already spoken extensively in New York, Pennsylvania, New England, and the Midwest.[4] By 1878, she had lectured in a total of twenty-one states, plus the District of Columbia.[5] She spoke out against the oppression of slaves and women across the country. Truth was a freedom fighter in every sense of the phrase.

Truth was accustomed to standing out in the crowd. The convention in Akron was no different. Truth looked different from the other women in more ways than just the color of her skin. On that day, as usual, she wore a plain gray dress, a white turban, and an unfashionable sunbonnet. Her style of dress did not match the fashions of the middle-class and upper-class white women gathered at the convention. Truth did not mind, though. She was not there to be fashionable. She was there to spread her message.[6]

Despite her unusual appearance, people could not help but be drawn to Truth. Her speeches were always moving. They often drew heavily on her own experiences as a slave. A devout Christian, Truth used biblical parables and Christian hymns in her talks. Many of her stories were very funny and almost always a bit sarcastic. At the same time, however, Truth was an extremely kind person. She referred to her listeners as "honey" and "child," and adapted an almost grandmotherly tone when speaking. Truth was no ordinary speaker. Even her adversaries were captivated by her unique style.

According to Gage, there were many women who opposed the idea of Truth's speaking at Akron and making the convention an "abolition affair." Some thought allowing an ex-slave and abolitionist such as Truth to speak might take attention away from women's rights issues. They begged Gage not to allow Truth to speak. To these objections, Gage simply answered, "We shall see when the time comes."[7]

On the first day of the convention, Truth quietly listened to the other lecturers. During intermissions she sold copies of her book, *The Narrative of Sojourner Truth*, which she published herself. Although Truth never learned to read or write, she had friends help her record the experiences of her life so that she could publish an autobiography. Because she was not as well-known as other abolitionists of the time, Truth

Y⁵ MAY SESSION OF Y⁵ WOMAN'S RIGHTS CONVENTION—Y⁵ ORATOR OF Y⁵ DAY DENOUNCING Y⁵ LORDS OF CREATION.

Women had begun to assemble to discuss women's rights issues several years before Truth's historic speech. Chief among the rights these women wanted to attain was suffrage—the right to vote.

sold her books at various conventions in order to make a living. Her sales in Akron that May were fairly successful.

According to Gage, there was a bit more excitement at the convention on the second day. Several of the men in the audience began making comments about what a real woman was. They argued that women were naturally weaker than men. They thought women needed help to do such simple activities as climbing in and out of carriages and walking over ditches. Some also brought up the issue of slavery, saying that whites were naturally the dominant race. When Truth heard these prejudiced comments against her gender and her race, she could no longer keep silent. She walked to the podium and began to speak in a voice that sounded "like rolling thunder":

> Nobody eber help me into carriages, or ober mud puddles, or gives me any best place . . . and ar'n't I a woman? Look at me! Look at my arm! . . . I have plowed and planted, and gathered into barns, and no man could head [beat] me—and ar'n't I a woman? I could work as much and eat as much as a man (when I could get it), and bear the lash as well—and ar'n't I a woman? I have borne thirteen chilern and seen 'em mos' all sold off into slavery, and when I cried out with a mother's grief, none but Jesus heard—and ain't I a woman?[8]

Gage's version of the speech exaggerated some aspects of Truth's life. For example, Truth had only five children, not thirteen. Also, Gage's version of Truth's speech was written in a stilted Southern dialect. Truth never lived in the South, and therefore, did not speak in such a manner. Gage probably wrote it in this way so that people would believe they were actually the words of an ex-slave, rather than a white abolitionist. In fact, many recent historians have argued convincingly that Gage edited most of Truth's speech to make it more dramatic. Most likely, it was Gage, not Truth, who coined the famous phrase,

Truth's famous speech tied together her experience as both a slave and a woman. She gave examples of what she had endured while enslaved to challenge the perception of what it meant to be a woman.

"Ain't I a woman?" Regardless of the precise words and the exaggeration of detail, though, the message was still clearly Sojourner Truth's.

Truth's message was historic because of the way she combined the issues of slavery and women's rights. She gave a new definition of womanhood in the nineteenth century. Truth's woman was not a helpless creature. She was strong, independent, and capable of doing anything as well as a man—much like Truth herself. Truth also spoke out against slavery. Mentioning her labor, her beatings, and her children being sold was her way of highlighting the evils of slavery. More than anything, though, Truth demonstrated her own strength, her fierce sense of independence, and her iron will. She would not let anyone tell her she was an inferior human being because she happened to be a black woman. Despite the many hardships she faced during her lifetime, Truth not only survived, she overcame.

CHAPTER ONE

EARLY LIFE AS A SLAVE

Sometime around 1797 a slave named Isabella was born in Hurley, New York. Her exact birthdate was never recorded because slaves' births were not considered important events. Isabella also had no last name. Her master was a man named Colonel Johannes Hardenbergh. Isabella was known simply as Hardenbergh's property. It would not be until much later in life that Isabella would be known by a new name of her own choosing—Sojourner Truth.

Colonel Hardenbergh owned a large estate in the rural town of Hurley, in Ulster County, New York. His Dutch ancestors had been some of the town's earliest settlers. He was one of the richest men in the county and owned about six or seven slaves.[1] Colonel Hardenbergh spoke English as well as a language called Low Dutch. He taught his slaves only Dutch—it was easier to control them if they could not communicate with anyone outside the estate.[2]

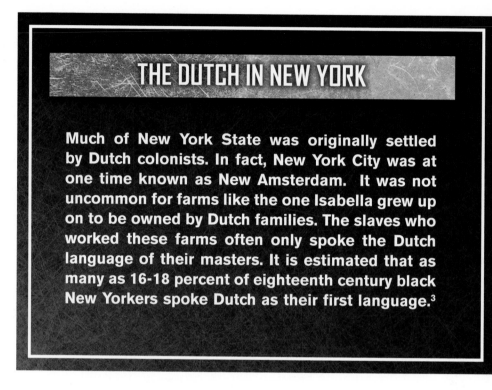

THE DUTCH IN NEW YORK

Much of New York State was originally settled by Dutch colonists. In fact, New York City was at one time known as New Amsterdam. It was not uncommon for farms like the one Isabella grew up on to be owned by Dutch families. The slaves who worked these farms often only spoke the Dutch language of their masters. It is estimated that as many as 16-18 percent of eighteenth century black New Yorkers spoke Dutch as their first language.[3]

PARENTS AND SIBLINGS

Isabella was somewhat lucky. Both of her parents, James and Elizabeth, were also owned by Colonel Hardenbergh. Many slaves were sold to different owners and never got to know their families. Isabella's father was very tall, straight, and strong. He was called Baumfree, which is a Dutch word that means *tree*. Isabella's mother, Elizabeth, was known as Mau-Mau Bett. She was Baumfree's third wife. His previous two wives had been sold away to other masters.

Before she was known as Sojourner Truth, the young slave called Isabella worked for Colonel Johannes Hardenbergh in this home in rural upstate New York. Hardenbergh owned Isabella's parents, as well.

Baumfree and Mau-Mau had between ten and twelve children. All but two of them were sold to different farms. Isabella and her brother Peter got to stay at the Hardenbergh estate. Because so many of her children were gone, Mau-Mau was often very sad. Sometimes Isabella would find her crying. When Isabella asked her mother what was wrong, she would say, "Oh my child, I am thinking of your brothers and sisters that have been taken away from me."[4] Mau-Mau constantly worried about the possibility of Peter and Isabella being taken away as well. Mau-Mau would often tell Isabella the story of her two older siblings to explain the pain and fear with which she lived.

One snowy morning, Mau-Mau's five-year-old son, Michael, had gone to gather some firewood. In the meantime, a sleigh arrived at the estate. At first, the child was delighted to see such a new sight. As he watched a strange man place his little sister Nancy on the sleigh, however, Michael began to get confused. His confusion soon turned to horror as he then saw the man shove Nancy into a small box, shut the lid, and lock it. Michael tried to run away

HOW TRUTH LEARNED THE BIBLE

Truth never learned to read or write, but she learned scriptures by heart by having them read to her. She did not like adults to read to her, however, because they often added their own commentary. "Children," Truth said, "would re-read the same sentence to her, as often as she wished, and without comment; and in that way, she was enabled to see what her own mind could make of the record . . . and not what others thought it to mean."[5]

but was quickly caught and secured on the sleigh. Michael and Nancy had been sold. They would never see their parents again. Baumfree and Mau-Mau could do nothing but watch helplessly as their children were stolen away from them.[6]

One of Mau-Mau's few comforts was her strong belief in God. After Mau-Mau's work was done for the day, she would gather her children and teach them her religious beliefs. Mau-Mau told her children that they could ask God for help whenever they fell into trouble.[7] Isabella took these teachings very seriously and held them sacred her entire life.

DEATH OF COLONEL HARDENBERGH

Isabella never knew Colonel Hardenbergh very well because he died when she was very young. His estate was left to his son, Charles. Slaves were considered part of the estate, so they, too, were inherited by Charles Hardenbergh. Hardenbergh decided to move his newly acquired slaves and livestock to a house he had built nearby.

With no slave quarters at his mansion, the slaves were forced to sleep in the cellar. All the slaves, both male and female, slept in the same room. There was no privacy. Each slave got only a little straw and a blanket as a bed. The room was very dark and damp. Sometimes, a hard rain would turn the dirt floor to mud. As a result of living in these conditions, many of the slaves were often sick.

In 1808, Isabella's second master became very ill. It was clear that he was dying. The slaves began to worry about what would happen to them after Charles Hardenbergh died. A few days later, they got their answer. After Charles Hardenbergh's funeral, his entire estate, including all of his slaves, was auctioned off. Nine-year-old Isabella would be separated from her beloved family.

By the time Charles Hardenbergh died, Baumfree was already very old. His arms and legs had become disfigured as a result of his years of labor and living in the damp cellar. The Hardenbergh family knew they would get no money for him if they sent him to auction. Essentially, he was valueless and useless to them. So they freed him.

In New York State, it was illegal to free slaves like Baumfree, who were no longer productive and had no means of fending for themselves. In an attempt to satisfy the law, the Hardenberghs also freed Mau-Mau, who, in theory, could take care of her husband. While Mau-Mau was certainly younger than Baumfree, it was still nearly impossible for her to provide for them both. Neither could speak English, nor did they have a way of earning a living in the outside world. The Hardenberghs told them they could continue living in the cellar if Mau-Mau agreed to continue working for the family. They had no choice but to accept the Hardenberghs' offer.

SOLD AT AUCTION

Meanwhile, Isabella and her brother Peter were put on the auction block. Isabella watched in horrified silence as Peter was sold to a man who lived very far away. Then it was her turn. At first, no one bid on Isabella. The auctioneer decided to throw in a flock of sheep to sweeten the deal. A man named John Nealy could not pass up such a bargain, so he bought Isabella and the sheep for a mere one hundred dollars.[8]

Nealy was a shopkeeper who also lived in Ulster County. He and his wife had recently moved from Massachusetts to New York. They did not get along well with the surrounding Dutch community. Perhaps this was because the Nealys only spoke English, while their neighbors

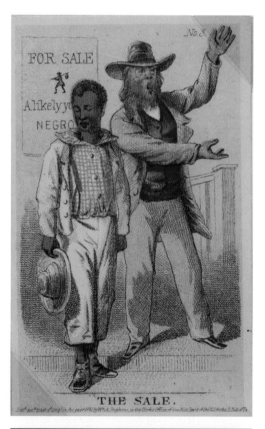

THE SALE.

Slaves were sold at auction to the highest bidder. This practice, no different than the selling of livestock and farm machinery, was dehumanizing.

mainly spoke Dutch. For Isabella, of course, the language barrier was a problem. How could she be expected to understand her English-speaking masters if she only knew Dutch?

Nealy's wife tried to teach young Isabella English, but she was a very impatient woman. Although Isabella tried to learn, it was never fast enough for her mistress. Mrs. Nealy would always end up screaming at the child or throwing things at her. At times, Mrs. Nealy would turn her husband against Isabella. The most memorable and painful instance was a day when Nealy used a burning hot rod to beat Isabella. The scars from that torturous beating stayed with her for the rest of her life.[9]

Even though she had been there less than a year, Isabella hated life at the Nealys' and she prayed to be rescued.[10] One winter day, after many weeks of waiting, Isabella's prayers were answered when her father came to visit her. At first, she could not tell him of her misery for fear they might be overheard. As Baumfree prepared to leave, Isabella walked him to the gate. She told him of her horrible mistress and showed him the scars on her back. He was horrified and promised to try to help his daughter.

Baumfree thought he could try to find a new master for Isabella, since slaves were sometimes able to help one another by finding out who the kinder masters were and then convincing them to buy their friends and family. Not long after seeing her father, Isabella learned that this was precisely what he had done for her.

Somehow, Baumfree convinced a fisherman named Martin Schriver to inquire about Isabella. Schriver lived about five miles from the Nealys. He came to their farm to ask Isabella if she would like to work for him instead. Isabella quickly agreed. She figured nothing could be worse than the Nealys. Schriver bought Isabella for $105.[11] Baumfree had kept his promise by rescuing his daughter from the awful Nealys.

A NEW MASTER

Life with the Schrivers was not as hard for Isabella as it had been at the Nealys. She spent many days outdoors, gardening, carrying fish, and even shopping at the local market. The Schrivers were not cruel like the Nealys and they did not beat Isabella. They also spoke both English and Dutch, so it was much easier for Isabella to understand them. Since no one was constantly yelling at her, Isabella was not under pressure to learn English and quickly picked up the language. In fact, Isabella learned it so well, she also picked up the bad habit of mildly cursing from time to time!

Working for the Schrivers was a vast improvement over life with the Nealys. Many of Isabella's duties were performed outside in the fresh air. She was even asked to shop at the local market.

While working for the Schrivers, Isabella received some painful news. Her mother, Mau-Mau, had died. Baumfree had come home one winter morning to find his wife lying on the floor. A few hours later, she died. It had simply been too cold in the cellar for the woman to live. Baumfree was overcome with grief. Isabella worried about how he would survive without his wife. A short time later, Isabella's worries were over. Baumfree, too, passed away. Without anyone to help take care of him, he had starved to death.[12]

Around the same time, a stranger visited the Schrivers' farm. His name was John Dumont. He was a farmer from New Paltz, New York. He offered to buy tall, strong Isabella from the Schrivers. For the third and last time in the thirteen-year-old's life, Isabella was sold. This time she was sold for about $175.[13]

JOHN DUMONT AND FAMILY

As far as slave owners went, Dumont was a fairly good man. He was not excessively cruel like the Nealys, but he did beat Isabella. Still,

Isabella was always very eager to please him. Dumont could not help but notice Isabella's hard work. He often bragged about Isabella, saying, she "is better to me than a *man*—for she will do a good family's washing in the night, and be ready in the morning to go into the field, where she will do as much at raking and binding as my best hands."[14]

While Isabella's ambition pleased her master, it was not looked upon so kindly by the other slaves. They did not understand how she could be so eager to please a man who kept her in captivity. The older slaves could not keep up with the young Isabella. Many were resentful of her for making them look bad, even if she did it unintentionally.[15]

Another person on the estate who was not happy with Isabella was Dumont's wife, Sally. Much like Mrs. Nealy, Mrs. Dumont was never satisfied with anything Isabella did and constantly yelled at her. While Mr. Dumont praised Isabella for the amount of work she did, Mrs. Dumont accused her of doing her jobs only half way. In 1812, though, these accusations proved false. In an incident involving a white servant girl named Kate and the Dumonts' ten-year-old daughter, Gertrude, Isabella proved Mrs. Dumont wrong.

One of Isabella's chores was to wash potatoes in the morning and boil them for breakfast. Isabella would scrub the potatoes as hard as she could in order to make certain that not one speck of dirt remained on them. Yet, somehow, there always remained an unusually large amount of dirt in the bottom of the pot of water. Isabella knew she had thoroughly cleaned the potatoes and could not understand how they could still be dirty. When Mrs. Dumont scolded Isabella for her carelessness, Gertrude defended her. Isabella was both surprised and happy to hear the Dumonts' daughter speak up for her. Together, the two young girls plotted to unravel the mystery of the dirty potatoes.

The next day, Isabella cleaned the potatoes and put them in the pot as usual. While Isabella went to milk the cows, Gertrude hid in the kitchen. As soon as Isabella left, the servant, Kate, came in and dumped ashes into the water. Gertrude ran off to tell her father what had really been happening to the potatoes. With the help of her new friend, Isabella was able to clear her name.[16]

CHAPTER TWO

A FREE WOMAN

With her parents dead and her siblings sold off, Isabella was often lonely. When she was around sixteen she thought her luck might have changed during a festival known as Pinxster. It was a favorite holiday amongst Dutch New York, as well as their slaves. For the slaves, Pinxster celebrated both African traditions and European customs. Celebrations could last for days.[1] During these festivities, Isabella met a man named Robert, a slave from a neighboring farm. They quickly fell in love. Unfortunately, Robert's master, Mr. Catlin, did not approve of the relationship. He wanted Robert to marry one of his own slaves. That way, any children they had would become Catlin's property.

Even though Catlin forbade Robert from seeing Isabella, the young man still visited her. One day, Catlin and his son discovered that Robert was missing and tracked him to the Dumonts' farm. When they found him, they began to beat him severely. As Robert lay on the ground bleeding, it looked like he might not live if they continued to hit and kick him.

Enslaved people did not enjoy the freedom of moving about as they pleased. Nor could they always fall in love with whomever they wanted. Robert was severely beaten just for sneaking out to visit his beloved, Isabella.

Dumont stopped the beating, telling Catlin and his son that he would have no slaves killed on his property. The two men collected Robert to take him home. Dumont followed them back to their farm to make sure they did not kill him on the way. Although Dumont had helped prevent Robert's murder that day, it was still the last day Isabella ever saw him.[2]

Soon after the incident with Robert, Dumont forced Isabella to marry one of his slaves, Thomas.

Her new husband had had two wives before her. Between about 1815 and 1826, Isabella had five children with Thomas—Diana, Peter, Elizabeth, Sophia, and Thomas. Isabella was happy to be a mother, even though it was hard work. Since she was, of course, still expected to work in the fields, Isabella would put an infant in a basket and tie it securely to a tree branch. With this makeshift hammock, Isabella was able to watch and rock her child while continuing to work.[3]

EMANCIPATION

During this time in Isabella's life, there was much happening to New York State's slavery laws. Many states in the North were passing laws to end slavery. Unlike the South, which claimed to need slaves to work huge cotton and tobacco plantations, most farmers in the North had small farms where they grew just enough for themselves and their families. The North was also developing an economy based on trade and industry, rather than agriculture alone. For these reasons, and because the North had thousands of immigrants arriving each year to work in the cities, slaveholders' excuses for upholding slavery were no longer valid. Many Northern states were taking steps to get rid of it entirely.

According to the New York state legislature, all slaves born after July 4, 1799, were "free." However, they had to remain as unpaid servants

Slavery was phased out in New York when its economy became dominated by industry and trade. Goods were shipped in and out of its busy ports daily.

until the age of twenty-nine for boys, and twenty-four for girls.[4] Because Isabella was born before 1799, only her children fell within the law. In 1817, all that changed. Under a new law passed by New York State, all slaves over the age of twenty-eight were to be freed by July 4, 1827. For Isabella, this new law meant that she would be a free woman in ten more years.

When Dumont heard about the law, he decided to do even more for Isabella, as a reward for her years of hard work. Dumont promised Isabella that he would free her one year early if she continued to work hard. So she worked twice as hard in order to earn her early emancipation. In the process,

Isabella hurt her right hand. At times, her injury made it painful and difficult to work. Even this hardship did not keep Isabella from trying her best, because she wanted so much to be free.

Finally, July 4, 1826, came. Isabella went to her master to remind him of his promise. To Isabella's surprise, Dumont refused to free her. He claimed that she had not worked hard enough as a result of her injured hand.

Isabella was very angry. She had always done her best for Dumont and now he was pretending otherwise. With typical determination, she decided to hold Dumont to his promise. Isabella worked hard for Dumont all during the summer of 1826 and even into the fall harvest season. Despite her anger, she did not want to leave him short-handed during the farm's busiest season.

One night in late fall 1826, Isabella felt she heard the voice of God telling her what to do. She bundled up only her infant daughter, Sophia, and packed up some food. With nothing else, Isabella left the Dumont estate and literally walked to free-dom. After walking for five miles, she ended up at the home of Levi Rowe, a Quaker and opponent of slavery. Rowe was very sick and could not help Isabella and her child himself. Instead, he told her to go to his friends, Isaac and Maria VanWagener. The VanWageners were also members of a local Dutch Reformed Church, and they strongly opposed slavery. When Isabella arrived at their

Runaway slaves attempted escape at great peril. Often times, they were traveling in unfamiliar territory. In addition, slave owners and bounty hunters were on their trail to capture and return them.

house and told them her story, they welcomed her into their home.

The next day, Dumont came looking for Isabella. When he found her at the VanWageners', he demanded that she return, but Isabella refused. Although the VanWageners opposed slavery, they wanted to avoid an unpleasant confrontation. They offered Dumont $25 for Isabella and her child. Dumont accepted.[5]

After Dumont left, Isabella thanked Mr. VanWagener, mistakenly thinking he was her new master. To this he replied, "there is but *one* master;

JOHN DUMONT

The last episode from the first edition of Truth's *Narrative* is not directly about her, but rather about the conversion of her old master, John Dumont. While visiting her daughter Diana in the spring of 1849, Truth stopped to speak with her old master. She was delighted to hear that, after many years, he had come to realize that slavery was evil. Dumont told Truth that "slavery was the wickedest thing in the world, the greatest curse the earth had ever felt–that it was then very clear to his mind that it was so, though, while he was a slaveholder himself, he did not see it so."[6]

and he who is your master is *my* master."[7] Isabella understood the religious meaning of his statement right away. Mr. VanWagener was telling Isabella that her only master was God. On hearing these words, Isabella realized that, for the first time in her life, she was free.

A SON IN PERIL

Isabella decided to stay and work for the VanWageners. Her life there was very satisfying, and she even took VanWagener for her last name. In a short time, however, Isabella discovered that her problems were far from over.

Before Isabella had left Dumont, her master had sold her son, Peter. At the VanWageners', Isabella received the troublesome news that her son had then been illegally sold south. Peter had originally been bought by a man named Dr. Gedney, who wanted to take him to England as a servant. After deciding Peter was too young to travel overseas, Dr. Gedney sold the boy to his brother Solomon. Solomon Gedney, in turn, broke New York state law by selling Peter to a farmer in Alabama named Fowler. Although slavery had been abolished in the North, it was still legal in the South. This meant that Peter might never be freed. As long as he was trapped in Alabama, he was in grave danger. Isabella was worried for the safety and future of her son, but she did not feel defeated.[8]

Isabella returned to the Dumonts'. She confronted her old master and mistress and demanded to know what had happened to her son. Mr. Dumont denied knowing anything about Gedney's actions. Mrs. Dumont laughed at Isabella for making such a fuss over a little black boy. Isabella started to leave, but then stopped. She turned and said in a very determined manner, "I have no money, but God has enough, or what's better! And I'll have my child again." In later remembering that day, Isabella said, "Oh my God! I know'd I'd have him agin. I was sure God would help me to get him. Why, I felt so *tall within*—I felt as if the *power of a nation* was with me!"[9]

Next, Isabella went to Mrs. Gedney, the mother of the man who had sold Peter to Fowler. Mrs. Gedney was just as unsympathetic as Mrs. Dumont had been. Mrs. Gedney's daughter Eliza was also in Alabama, and she complained to Isabella that she missed her child just as much as Isabella missed hers. Isabella realized it was useless trying to talk to this woman. Before she left, Isabella pointed out that, while Eliza was in Alabama, she was free. Peter had been dragged illegally against his will, and was in danger of remaining a slave for the rest of his life.[10]

Determined as ever, Isabella returned to the VanWageners for help. They sent her to the nearby town of Kingston. Once in Kingston, Isabella met some Quaker abolitionists who offered to help. Quakers were members of a branch of Christianity that strongly opposed slavery. They told her how to find the county courthouse and suggested that she file a complaint against Gedney. They also helped Isabella pay her legal fees.

Members of the Quaker sect were adamant abolitionists. They vehemently opposed the enslavement of other people. Escaped slaves were often aided to freedom by Quakers.

Isabella filed a complaint against Solomon Gedney for unlawfully taking her son south. The case was brought before a grand jury. Surprisingly, the jury decided in her favor, even though she was a black woman bringing suit against a white man—a rare occurrence at that time. After many legal complications, papers were finally served to Gedney, ordering him to return Peter.

At first, Peter did not want to go back to his mother. Peter was now legally free, but because he had been separated from her for over a year, he was confused about where he belonged. After a little while, Isabella was able to convince him that she was his mother and he belonged with her.

Once Peter agreed, Isabella was able to get her first good look at her son. She was horrified to discover that Peter was scarred from head to toe. Fowler had repeatedly whipped, kicked, and beaten Peter until his tiny body was virtually maimed as a result. Although Isabella knew there was nothing she could do about the old scars, she knew that Peter would never be beaten like that again. Isabella thanked God for returning her son and swore that no child of hers would ever be taken away again.[11]

Isabella was so happy to have her son back that she did not grasp the full magnitude of what she had just achieved. In her fight to win back her child, Isabella had become one of the first blacks in the country to sue a white person successfully. For the first, but certainly not the last, time, Isabella had made history.

CHAPTER THREE

A MOVE TO NEW YORK CITY

Isabella and Peter returned to the Kingston area and continued to live with the VanWageners. She earned a living doing housework. Although she was pleased to be free and earning her own way, she missed her other children. Most were still slaves at the Dumonts' farm. Isabella reached out to her old master in hopes he would let her visit. Dumont agreed, and Isabella was allowed to regularly connect with her children on the estate.

While living with the VanWageners, Isabella became very serious about the Methodist religion. She regularly attended church services and meetings. At one of these meetings Isabella met a white school teacher named Miss Grear. Miss Grear grew fond of Isabella and especially of young Peter. Grear was on her way back to New York City and suggested that Isabella and her son join her. In New York, there would be more educational opportunities for Peter, and Grear could help Isabella find a better housekeeping job with a family she knew.[1]

There were also many other free blacks in the city—
a prospect that appealed to Isabella.

Isabella considered what reasons she might
have to stay. She did not have to worry about her
husband. Thomas had been freed on July 4, 1827.
Like Isabella, he worked wherever he could find
jobs, but times were harder on Thomas than on
Isabella. He never made enough money to survive and he died in debt less than a year after his
emancipation.[2] Their children were still slaves at
the Dumonts'. They would not be freed for several
years, until each reached the age of twenty-four.

After living in the country all her life, Isabella was shocked by the
chaos of New York City. Still, she was convinced the city offered
more opportunities to her and her son Peter.

After taking all these facts into consideration, Isabella decided it would be better for her and Peter to move to New York City. Peter had been getting into trouble lately, lying and even stealing. She hoped New York City would give them a fresh start, away from the environment where slavery had plagued both their lives.

ADJUSTING TO LIFE IN THE CITY

Life in the city was dramatically different from the country life of Ulster County. Instead of sprawling farms, Isabella saw tightly packed buildings lining cobblestone streets. The streets were crowded with horse-drawn carriages and people constantly moving. New York was not a city that ever stood still! The unfamiliar sights and sounds must have been somewhat confusing and even frightening for newcomers. After a time, though, Isabella became accustomed to New York and learned to navigate the busy streets along with everyone else.

Grear helped Isabella find work as a servant in the homes of some family and friends. After finding a job and a place to live, the next important task for Isabella was to find a church. At first, she attended the John Street Church, a Methodist congregation. She did not feel comfortable there, though, mainly because services were segregated. She soon changed to the Mother Zion African Methodist Episcopal (AME) Church. The AME Church had an all-black congregation and Isabella felt at home there. In fact, the church would prove to be more like a home than Isabella could possibly imagine.

CHURCH AND FAMILY

When Isabella was still in Ulster County, she had established contact with her sister Sophia, who lived in New York. After her move, Isabella and her sister got to meet face-to-face. Sophia told Isabella that their brother Michael was also living in the city. Isabella had never met Michael, but she remembered her mother's story about him and their sister. During their first meeting, Isabella anxiously asked about Nancy, Mau-Mau's other child who had been carried away in the sleigh. Michael explained that Nancy had been living in New York but had passed away a few months earlier. Michael described her and mentioned that she had been a member of the AME Church as well. As Michael spoke of Nancy, Isabella realized she had met her at church without even knowing who she was. Isabella remembered being "struck with the peculiar feeling of her hand— the bony hardness so just like mine? and yet I could not know she was my sister; and now I see she looked *so* like my mother." Isabella, Sophia, and Michael wept, and Isabella wondered to herself "what is this slavery, that it can do such dreadful things."[3]

Through people she knew at church, Isabella became a volunteer at the Magdalene House of

Refuge— a shelter for homeless women, run by a man named Elijah Pierson. Isabella came to know Pierson through his black servant, Katy. Eventually, Isabella took over the housekeeping position when Katy left to visit her children. Pierson was not just Isabella's employer, he was also a religious mentor. Many of Pierson's religious views were similar to Isabella's, so she found it easy to follow his leadership. Pierson's religious beliefs eventually took an extreme turn. He began telling people that he was a prophet of God.

While Isabella was working at Pierson's, a stranger came to the door. He was a striking man with long hair, a beard, and piercing eyes.[4] Isabella's first impression was that this man might be Jesus Christ himself. Actually, he was a con artist named Robert Matthews. He went by the name Matthias, and would change Isabella's life forever.

THE KINGDOM

Together, Pierson and Matthias formed what they claimed was a religious "community," they called

Isabella found a church in New York City, the Mother Zion AME church. During this time, such churches were havens from the world that oppressed African Americans and focused on all concerns of the black community.

the Kingdom. Nowadays the Kingdom would be regarded as a cult. The Kingdom advocated equality for all, regardless of race, sex, class, or age, and proclaimed that "our creed is truth."[5] Despite warnings from her family and friends that Matthias was an imposter, Isabella was attracted by the egalitarian idea of his Kingdom. She agreed to join the community, along with several other very religious Methodists. Along with the other members, she willingly gave Matthias all her hard-earned money. The group brought their possessions together and moved to a communal house in Sing Sing, New York.

Isabella thought she would be an equal in this community, despite being the only black person. Nonetheless, she always ended up doing most of the cooking and cleaning. She was also often asked to leave the room when important decisions were being made.[6] These problems turned out to be minor compared to other happenings within the community.

Matthias now proclaimed himself to be Jesus personified, and Pierson claimed to be John the Baptist. Although the Kingdom was supposedly based on equality, Matthias was clearly in charge. He made all the decisions for the Kingdom and instituted strange policies such as communal bathing and free love. In addition, Matthias had control over all the finances of the Kingdom.[7] The community members were asked to give all their worldly possessions to the Kingdom. Isabella herself continued to give all the money she had, plus several pieces of furniture. Matthias must have used most of the money on himself—he was always dressed in fine clothing and his table was always spread with wonderful foods.[8]

Controversy in the Kingdom continued when Pierson mysteriously died in 1834. The circumstances surrounding his death became even more bizarre when Matthias was accused of poisoning him. As if that were not enough, two members of the Kingdom, Ann and Benjamin Folger, accused Isabella of witchcraft, as well as of trying to poison them. The Kingdom of Matthias was collapsing and it seemed Isabella was going down with it.

As usual, Isabella would not give up without a fight. She once again turned to the courts to help with her problems. Isabella sued the Folgers for slander—making false accusations that ruined her good name. For a second time, Isabella won a lawsuit against white people. She was awarded a small amount of money for the Folgers' lies. Isabella also agreed to tell her side of the story to a reporter named Gilbert Vale. In 1835, Vale published a book entitled *Fanaticism, Its Sources and Influence*, in order to help Isabella clear her name.[9]

Matthias was also eventually acquitted of Pierson's murder. Exposed as an imposter, he moved out west and died alone six years later.

A Great Awakening occurred in America in the first half of the nineteenth century. During this time, millions of people were converted to Christianity. Those in charge were often con artists much like Robert Matthews, aka Matthias.

TROUBLE WITH PETER

As a result of her involvement with the Kingdom and the lawsuit, Isabella had not been able to keep a careful eye on Peter. During her absence, her teenage son had dropped out of school and started hanging out with a dangerous group. Isabella tried to discipline him upon her return but had little success. Peter continually wound up in jail and his mother would always bail him out. Finally, Isabella warned her son that she would no longer help him if he continued to get into trouble. Peter did not believe his mother until he was once again thrown in jail for theft. This time, Isabella refused to help. Though it pained her to do so, she felt it was in his best interest.

Peter was a clever boy, and although he was trapped in jail, he quickly thought of a plan of action. Peter often used the alias Peter Williams when he committed crimes. Since he was already stuck in jail, he decided to send for the *real* Peter Williams to ask for help. Williams was a respectable New York businessman. Surprisingly, he agreed to come to Peter's aid. Williams's help was not necessarily free, however. He told Peter he would help on the condition that Peter clean up his act and leave New York. Peter agreed. The next day, Williams helped Peter get a job aboard a whaling ship. At that time, working aboard a ship was considered a means of disciplining unruly young men. Peter left in the summer of 1839. Isabella did not hear from him until the fall of the following year, when she received the following letter, dated October 17, 1840:

> My Dear Beloved Mother:
> I take this opportunity to write to you and inform you that I am well, and in hopes for to find you the same. I am got on board the same unlucky ship Done, of Nantucket. I am sorry for to say, that I have been punished once severely. . . . We have had bad luck, but in hopes to have better. . . . Mother, I hope you do not forget me. . . . I hope you all will forgive me for all that I have done.
> Your son, PETER VAN WAGENER[10]

Touched by her son's letter, Isabella dictated a letter back almost immediately. The two kept in contact until September 1841, when Isabella received a fifth and final letter from her son. After that date, Isabella never heard from or about Peter again.[11]

THE BEGINNING OF SOJOURNER TRUTH

By the early 1840s, Isabella was very disappointed with life in New York City. The Matthias scandal had humiliated her and the loss of her son had left

LOOKING FOR A PLACE TO STAY

Isabella left New York without any idea where she was going or where she would sleep at night. In her *Narrative*, she recounted wandering from inn to inn, asking if she might stay the night, and always receiving a negative answer. Finally, she came to a large building that "was occupied as court-house, tavern, and jail." She was told she could stay, provided she did not mind being locked into one of the unoccupied cells. Tired as she was, she refused without a second thought. She continued on her way, "preferring to walk beneath the open sky, to being locked up by a stranger in such a place."[12]

her heartbroken. Conditions in New York were also very poor for free blacks. Isabella realized that she had been working for nearly seven years since she had given her money to Matthias, yet still had virtually nothing to show for it. She came to the sad conclusion that New York was a place where "the rich rob the poor, and the poor rob one another," so she decided to leave.[13]

On the morning of June 1, 1843, Isabella later said, she felt the voice of God telling her to travel and spread his word.[14] The woman who left that morning decided that the slave name Isabella was no longer acceptable for one of God's free pilgrims. Considering the nature of her journey, she decided on Sojourner, a synonym for traveler. For a last name, she eventually chose "Truth," probably as a reminder of the quest for truth that would guide the rest of her life. On June 1, 1843, Sojourner Truth began her journey.

CHAPTER FOUR

JOINING THE ABOLITIONISTS

I n the 1840s, it had become very popular for groups of religious people to gather and camp in wagons and tents to pray and to listen to religious lecturers. The newly named Sojourner Truth found these meetings to be an ideal place to fulfill her new mission. She became a regular fixture at these venues, getting up in front of large crowds to preach about God and religion. With practice and time, Truth would also begin to incorporate stories about her life as a slave as well.

A UNIQUE SPEAKING STYLE

Sojourner Truth was unlike most speakers of the day in more ways than one. Crowds would be transfixed by the physically imposing woman and her powerful stories. At times, she would make audiences laugh with her sarcastic sense of humor. Other times, she would bring the crowd to tears with her stories about slavery. Truth also made certain to include in her lectures hymns that she had written herself. Because of her unique style and unwavering faith, she became a favorite at many camp meetings.[1] She was often invited to come backand was recommended to speak at other meetings. In fact, Truth was so popular that she was able to make a living through her speaking tours.

Truth was usually the only black person at these meetings, a fact that did not bother her. Once in a while, though, Truth feared for her safety. On one occasion, a group of rowdy young men was disturbing a camp meeting by rudely interrupting speakers while they preached. At first, Truth ran to hide, thinking they might attack her for being black. After stopping a moment, Truth changed her mind. "Shall I run away and hide from the Devil?" she thought. "Have I not faith enough to go out and quell [quiet] that mob? . . . I'll go to the rescue, and the Lord shall go with and protect me."[2]

With that simple thought, Truth came out from her hiding place and began to sing in a loud, clear voice. The young men rushed toward her. Truth stopped her singing and asked why they wanted to hurt her. They replied that they did not want to hurt her, but rather, wanted to hear more of her stories and singing. Truth consented, so long as the young men would leave peacefully when she was done. They agreed and eventually left quietly. True to her word, Truth had calmed the crowd.[3]

EXPOSURE TO ABOLITIONISM

Truth's travels led her to Springfield, Massachusetts, where she was once again involved with religious camp meetings. In Springfield, some friends of Truth's suggested that she go live at the Northampton Association of Education and Industry in Northampton, Massachusetts.[4] The Northampton Association was a cooperative farm where members worked together to produce silk from silkworms.

Unlike Matthias's Kingdom, the community at Northampton was truly a cooperative one. The founders insisted "that every laborer be a partner in the enterprise, filled with the spirit of ownership and participation."[5] This emphasis on equality was important in all aspects of the Northampton Association, and the community soon became well known for its tolerance of all people, regardless of race, gender, religion, or class. It also happened to be one of the country's foremost centers for the abolition movement. At the Northampton Association, Truth met many prominent abolitionists and public intellectuals. She had finally found a community that truly promoted human equality.

Among the abolitionists visiting Northampton was the famous William Lloyd Garrison. Garrison had become involved in the abolition movement at a young age. In 1831, when he was only twenty-six years old, he launched *The Liberator*, one of

Journalist William Lloyd Garrison became a key figure in both the abolitionist movement and the women's rights movement. His newspaper *The Liberator* was dedicated to turning people against slavery.

the most influential antislavery newspapers in the country. In addition to editing *The Liberator*, Garrison was cofounder and president of the American Anti-Slavery Society, which worked to eliminate slavery in the United States.

WILLIAM LLOYD GARRISON AND WOMEN'S RIGHTS

William Lloyd Garrison was not only one of the most radical abolitionists of his day, but amongst the most vocal in pointing out the connections between the anti-slavery movement and the women's rights movement. At the first World's Anti-Slavery Convention held in London in 1840, many men argued against women of any color or background being able to participate. Garrison took a hard stance in arguing on behalf of women being allowed to attend. "After battling so many long years for the liberties of African slaves, I can take no part in a convention that strikes down the rights of all women. All of the slaves are not men."[6] The eventual compromise reached was to allow women to attend as spectators, but not participate directly. While they could listen, their seating was relegated to a curtained off area at one end of the gallery. In protest, Garrison and others gave up their seats on the main floor to sit in solidarity with the women attendees.

Another resident of Northampton was David Ruggles, a black man who had been born free in Connecticut but had dedicated his life to the abolition movement. He contributed publicly by writing for an antislavery journal called *The Mirror of Liberty*. But it was Ruggles's underground contribution that directly helped slaves. Ruggles was the secretary of the New York Vigilance Committee—a secret organization that helped hundreds of runaway slaves escape from the South to freedom in the North.

Ruggles's position as a conductor of the Underground Railroad put him in personal danger, especially after passage of new fugitive slave laws. In 1793, Congress passed the Fugitive Slave Act, which allowed slaveholders to recapture runaway slaves. The law also said that people helping runaways were subject to a fine. Before 1850, however, this law was more or less ignored by abolitionists, and thousands of slaves were able to escape through the work of the Underground Railroad.

Approximately 100,000 slaves escaped through the network of secret escape routes and hiding places known as the Underground Railroad. Ushering slaves to freedom carried its own danger.

After 1850, helping escaped slaves became a much more dangerous activity with the passage of a stricter Fugitive Slave Act. The law was passed as part of the famous Compromise of 1850. In order to satisfy both antislavery Northerners and slave-holding Southerners, Congress agreed to admit California to the Union as a free state in order to make Northerners happy, but also agreed to update the 1793 Fugitive Slave Act for Southerners. This new law increased controversy between the North and the South. Many Northerners did not want any part of supporting slavery, nor did they agree with

HARRIET TUBMAN

Another famous conductor of the Underground Railroad was Harriet Tubman. She was born a slave in Maryland but escaped to the North in 1849. She made many trips back to the South, helping close to three hundred slaves escape. Tubman even used her own house in Auburn, New York, as a station on the escape route. Because of her work in freeing slaves from bondage, she became known as the Moses of her people, after the biblical hero who freed the Jews from bondage in Egypt.

the severity of the new law. The new law stated that a person only had to match a description of a runaway slave for a federal marshal to make an arrest. Of course, since blacks were not considered citizens, they were not allowed the right to defend themselves, let alone the right to a trial if they were wrongly dragged down south. In addition, the 1850 law increased the fine for anyone caught aiding a runaway from $500 to $1,000 or $2,000, and added possible imprisonment to the penalty.[7]

PRACTICAL ILLUSTRATION OF THE FUGITIVE SLAVE LAW.

This political cartoon shows the fight between northern abolitionists and those who supported the 1850 Fugitive Slave Act. William Lloyd Garrison is seen protecting a slave and pointing a gun at a slave catcher.

FREDERICK DOUGLASS

One of the most famous escapees of the Underground Railroad was also a frequent guest at the Northampton Association. His name was Frederick Douglass. Although Douglass was just beginning his career during the Northampton years, he would become one of the nineteenth century's greatest black leaders. Like Truth, Douglass was born a slave. After his mistress taught him the letters of the alphabet, Douglass taught himself to read and write.[8] In 1837, he used those skills to help himself escape to freedom. Douglass saw illiteracy as a link to enslavement, so he took great pains to educate and refine himself into an articulate spokesperson for the abolition movement.

Around the time Douglass first came to Northampton, he published his autobiography, which detailed his life as a slave as well as his escape. The publicity of the book put Douglass in danger of being recaptured, because he was still considered a runaway. He fled to England, because slavery had already been abolished throughout the British Empire. Eventually, some fellow abolitionists bought his freedom, and Douglass was able to return to the United States.

Although Truth made no mention of her time with Douglass at Northampton, he made sure to mention her in a pamphlet he published about the Association:

I met here for the first time that strange compound of wit and wisdom of wild enthu-siasm and flint-like common sense, who seemed to feel it her duty to trip me up in my speeches and to ridicule my efforts to speak and act like a person of cultivation and refinement. I allude to Sojourner Truth. . . . She cared very little for elegance of speech or refinement of manner. She seemed to please herself and others best when she put her ideas in the oddest forms. She was much respected . . . for she was honest, industri-ous, and amiable. Her quaint speeches easily gave her an audience, and she was one of the most useful members of the Community in its day of small things.[9]

In his pamphlet, Douglass pointed out the differ-ences between his and Truth's styles of speaking. According to him, his style was refined, while Truth's was plain. Despite their differences, how-ever, Douglass showed how respected and valued Truth was at Northampton.

At Northampton, Truth found not only a support-ive community where she learned more about the worlds of abolition and social reform. It expanded the scope and focus of her speaking to include these topics. Even after the farm closed in 1846, Truth remained in contact with other members of

Perhaps the most famous African-American abolitionist, Frederick Douglass's autobiographies educated many Americans about the horrors of slavery. His impressive writing and oratory skills proved that blacks were not inferior.

the community, often lecturing and traveling with them. Many of the abolitionists were Truth's friends as well as colleagues. In fact, upon the closing of the farm, one of the founders, Samuel Hill, offered to lend Truth the $300 she needed to buy her own house in the area.

THE NARRATIVE OF SOJOURNER TRUTH

Although Frederick Douglass's autobiography may have put him in danger, it also became very widely read among abolitionists and was one of the most important texts of the abolition movement. On a more practical level, it was also very profitable for Douglass. The book sold forty-five hundred copies in less than six months.[10] Keeping this in mind, a friend from the Northampton Association named Olive Gilbert suggested that Truth publish her own autobiography. Not only would it be a means of illustrating the horrors of slavery and advancing the abolition movement, but it would also help Truth raise the money to pay back Hill for her house.

Truth began dictating her story to Gilbert in 1850, less than one year after Douglass published his autobiography. The fact that the *Narrative* was dictated, rather than written by Truth, emphasizes that there will never be a completely authoritative way of knowing exactly what Truth said or thought. Gilbert's editorial role in Truth's *Narrative* explains inaccuracies, such as why much of Truth's dialogue is written in a Southern dialect she never used in real life. Nonetheless, *The Narrative of Sojourner Truth* is a valuable source of information about her life up until 1849. Truth would later reprint the *Narrative* several times to include events that occurred after that date.

Since she already had someone to write her story, the next step for Truth was to find a publisher. Her friend William Lloyd Garrison offered to help publish the book. He put Truth in contact with a printer he knew. Garrison even wrote a promotional endorsement for Truth in the May 1850 edition of *The Liberator*.[11] Garrison no doubt saw the value of Truth's story, especially since it was unique in the fact that Truth was born a slave in the North rather than the South. It also provided a woman's per-spective on and experience in slavery.

The Narrative of Sojourner Truth was printed on credit in 1850. Truth was not as well-known as Frederick Douglass, so her book was not circulated quite as much as his. This did not bother Truth. She simply began selling her own books whenever she went to abolition meetings. Eventually, she was able to save enough money to pay for the printing of the book, and more importantly, to pay for her house. At the age of fifty-seven, Truth had fulfilled one of her lifelong dreams—owning her own home.

CHAPTER FIVE

WOMEN'S RIGHTS ADVOCATE

As Truth became more involved with the abolitionists, she also began to get a taste for the women's rights movement. Like many abolitionists, Truth realized that women's rights activists were fighting for the same basic rights as those opposed to slavery. Many female abolitionists as well as some men crusaded for women's rights. In fact, Truth's Northampton associates, William Lloyd Garrison and Frederick Douglass, were both outspoken on the subject. Garrison included a special "Ladies Department" in his famous newspaper, *The Liberator*. He also made certain to point out in his speeches that slaves included black women.[1] As for Douglass, he was the only male to contribute to the first women's rights convention, held in Seneca Falls, New York, in 1848.

THE SENECA FALLS CONVENTION

The Seneca Falls Convention was organized by some of the most influential women's rights activists in the country, including Elizabeth Cady Stanton and Lucretia Mott. Stanton was probably the best-known advocate of women's rights in the nineteenth century. She fought tirelessly for women's rights and pushed for such changes as co-education, birth control, property rights for women, equal wages, and divorce law reform.[2] Stanton fought especially hard for women's right to vote. Without the right to vote, it was nearly impossible for women to make their voices heard in government. Stanton was chosen as the first president of the National Woman Suffrage Association in 1869. With the help of Susan B. Anthony, another famous activist, she compiled an impressive six-volume *History of Woman Suffrage* in order to document the women's suffrage movement.

Another influential woman who helped organize the Seneca Falls convention was Lucretia Mott. Mott was a Quaker schoolteacher from New York. She first became involved in the women's rights movement when she discovered that she was being paid less for doing the same work as her male colleagues. She and her husband, James, were also outspoken abolitionists. Lucretia Mott served as president of the American Anti-Slavery Association for several years.[3] Truth recognized the tireless work of Mott in a later edition of her *Narrative*. She called Mott "a woman whose four-score years are so replete with good words and deeds that the name falls like a benediction upon

Elizabeth Cady Stanton was an organizer of the women's rights movement in the United States. Stanton began her career in activism as an abolitionist before focusing on women's rights. Sojourner Truth worked with Stanton in the fight to attain women's suffrage.

the listening ear.... We involuntarily bow our hearts in worship when the honored name of Lucretia Mott is pronounced."[4]

The convention Mott and Stanton organized, which was held July 19 and 20, 1848, was a gathering of women to discuss the issues most important to their cause. These issues included the social, civil, and religious conditions that affected women of the nineteenth century. On the first day, the women simply spoke among themselves. On the second day, the women decided to put their ideas down in writing, drafting the famous "Declaration of Sentiments." The document was based on the Declaration of Independence, but the

THE MOTTS

Lucretia and James Mott were not always popular for their views. One time, a mob that did not agree with their liberal politics formed and began moving toward their house. A quick-thinking friend pretended to be a member of the mob and led the violent group in the opposite direction. The mob was so confused at not being able to find the Motts' house that it broke up and did not return.

women of Seneca Falls revised the original to say that all men *and* women are created equal.

Although Stanton, Mott, and the other organizers thought the convention was a great success, only about three hundred people actually made it to Seneca Falls.[5] However, press coverage brought the event to national attention. Many male newspaper reporters and editors were upset that women were calling openly for equal rights. They accused women's rights activists of being unfeminine and called their behavior improper. One newspaper

This illustration depicts the signing of a women's declaration of independence at a women's convention. It may be a nod to the presentation and signing of the Declaration of Sentiments at the Seneca Falls convention.

account went so far as to say that the convention was "the most shocking and unnatural incident ever recorded in the history of womanity."[6] In their attempts to belittle these women, though, such newspaper accounts gave the movement lots of free publicity. News of the Seneca Falls Convention and the Declaration of Sentiments spread well beyond the three hundred people present at the convention.

THE WORCESTER CONVENTION

Another meeting that received a lot of negative press coverage was the first national women's rights convention, held in Worcester, Massachusetts, in October 1850. This meeting was much larger than the Seneca Falls gathering, and more speakers, including Truth, were invited to give lectures.

At first, Truth quietly listened as other women took turns speaking. Finally, it was Truth's turn. She walked up to the podium and simply asked, "Sisters, I a'n't clear what you'd be after. Ef women want any rights more'n dey's got, why don't dey jus' take 'em an' not be talkin' about it?"[7] Truth thought that it was ridiculous that women should have to fight for rights. To her, it seemed obvious that men and women should have the same rights.

At the Worcester Convention, Truth saw her old friend Garrison. When it was over, he invited Truth to come on a speaking tour with him and a British abolitionist named George Thompson. Garrison thought it would be a good opportunity for Truth to sell more of her books. He also knew that Truth's powerful public speaking was sure to be an asset to the tour. Truth was always interested in selling more copies of her *Narrative*, but she did not have the money to go. Truth expressed her financial concerns to her friend. Generously, Garrison offered to pay Truth's expenses. All she had to do was meet him and Thompson in Springfield, Massachusetts.

When Truth arrived in Springfield a few months later, she learned that Garrison had fallen ill. He would not be touring with them. But Thompson still wanted Truth to be part of the tour. He asked her to continue with him, despite her friend's absence. Truth explained her financial arrangement with Garrison and said she could not afford to go without his help. Thompson assured Truth that he would be happy to pay her expenses. Truth accepted. Clearly, she was a valued member of the movement and people went to great lengths to include her. Truth and Thompson traveled throughout the Northeast, spreading their abolitionist message. According to Truth's recollections, this was sometimes difficult. Truth remembered that the lectures were often broken up by angry mobs. Nevertheless, Truth stood her ground and continued to preach.

By early spring, Truth and Thompson had traveled extensively. They eventually wound up in Rochester, New York. There, Truth met Isaac and

Amy Post, two prominent Quaker abolitionists. The Posts' beliefs about equality and racial tolerance, as well as religion, were similar to Truth's. They often offered Truth spiritual guidance during her stays with them.[8] Amy Post was also a leading figure in the women's rights movement. She had helped organize the 1848 Seneca Falls Convention. Perhaps because of all their similar interests, she and Truth became close friends and would correspond for most of Truth's life.

THE AKRON CONVENTION SPEECH

Truth stayed with the Posts for several months. By winter's end, though, she once again felt a call to travel. This time she was being called west. Truth heard that the second women's rights convention was to be held in Akron, Ohio, in May 1851. A famous antislavery newspaper called the *Anti-Slavery Bugle* invited "all the friends of Reform, in whatever department engaged" to attend.[9] Truth knew she had to be there.

It was at this convention that Truth made her famous "Ain't I a Woman" speech, which combined the two great struggles of her life—abolition and women's rights. As she proudly walked up to the podium, Truth made her presence known as an African American and as a woman. She made it clear that the women's rights movement should not exclude blacks, nor should the abolitionists exclude women. In other words, Sojourner Truth believed that neither racism nor sexism should be tolerated. Truth's "Ain't I a Woman" speech later became immortalized when Frances Gage published a version of it in the April 23, 1863, issue of the New York *Independent* newspaper. It was reprinted again in the 1870s in Truth's updated *Narrative*.

After Akron, Truth continued lecturing in the Midwest. She borrowed a horse and buggy from friends and spent the next two years traveling, lecturing, and selling her book.[10]

EXPERIENCES ON TOUR

It was not long after the Akron Convention that Truth once again brought attention to herself and her causes. In 1852, in Salem, Ohio, Truth was listening to Frederick Douglass speak at an anniversary meeting of an antislavery society. Douglass was growing frustrated with the slow progress of the abolition movement. Going against a philosophy of peaceful resolution, Douglass suggested that violence might be the only way to end black oppression. At this, Truth immediately jumped up from the audience and asked her colleague, "Frederick, *is God dead?*"[11] Even at the worst of times, Sojourner Truth did not lose faith in her beliefs, nor would she accept violence as a possible solution.

During another lecture in her Midwest tour, Truth was heckled by a man in the audience. He accused her of not supporting the Constitution of the United States. With a sparkle in her eye, Truth told a story to set the man straight. It revolved around a kind of beetle, called a weevil, that had ruined the wheat crop in Ohio that year.

"Children," she said,
I talk to God and God talks to me. I go out and talk to God in the fields and the woods. This morning I was walking out, and I got

SELLING THE SHADOW

As Truth's fame grew, she decided to add to her publicity through another means—photographs. During the late 1850s and 1860s, it was very popular to buy and sell small postcards with people's pictures on them. They were called "cartes de visites." Truth had several cards of herself made up with the phrase "I sell the shadow to support the substance" printed on the bottom. The slogan explained why Truth was selling the cards in the first place—to support herself during her crusade against slavery. She sold them at meetings along with her book.[12]

over the fence. I saw the wheat holding up its head, looking very big. I go up and take hold of it. You believe it, there was *no* wheat there? I say "God, what *is* the matter with *this* wheat?" And he says to me, "Sojourner, there is a little weevil in it."

Now I hear talking about this Constitution and the rights of man. I come up and I take hold of this Constitution. It looks *mighty big*, and I feel for *my* rights, but there ain't any there. Then I say "God, what *ails* this Constitution?" He says to me, "Sojourner, there is a little weevil in it."[13]

Through humor, Truth pointed out a fault in the Constitution—namely that it did not truly provide for the rights of *all* people.

I Sell the Shadow to Support the Substance.
SOJOURNER TRUTH.

This is one of Sojourner Truth's carte de visites. Sales of the cards supported Truth and her fight for equality.

THE LIBYAN SIBYL

By 1853, Truth was ready to head east. On her way back to her house in

Northampton, Truth decided to stop by the home of a very influential author of the time—Harriet Beecher Stowe. Stowe was the author of *Uncle Tom's Cabin, or Life Among the Lowly*, written in 1852. It is the story of a slave named Tom and the hardships he endures under his cruel master, Simon Legree. Stowe decided to write the novel in response to the harsh Fugitive Slave Law of 1850. The novel was extremely influential in opening people's eyes to the true horrors of slavery. It was also a huge commercial success. In the first week of publication, the book sold ten thousand copies![14]

As the story goes, Truth appeared one day at Stowe's home in Andover, Massachusetts. Stowe had a house full of company that day but was very taken with Truth. Stowe would later write, "I do not recollect ever to have been conversant with any one who had more of that silent and subtle power which we call personal presence than this woman." In fact, Stowe was so impressed that she invited Truth to come inside and join her guests. The group talked for hours about Truth's life, adventures, and most of all, her famous opinions. Truth even sang some of her hymns for them. As Stowe said, "no princess could have received a drawing-room with more composed dignity than Sojourner her audience."[15]

Before Truth left, she asked Stowe to sign her *Book of Life*. The *Book of Life* was Truth's collection of newspaper clippings and autographs of famous people she met on her journeys. It was later reprinted in a new edition of the *Narrative*.

Stowe eventually did much more for Truth than simply sign her book. Ten years later, Stowe wrote an article recounting her meeting with Truth. The essay, called "The Libyan Sibyl," appeared in the April 1863 issue of the famous magazine *Atlantic Monthly*. In addition to the story of their meeting, Stowe's article also contained biographical information on Truth. Most importantly, it increased Truth's fame and helped her cement the reputation she had already begun building for herself.

RESPONDING TO NAYSAYERS

Women of all backgrounds often faced adversity when speaking publicly about their cause. As a black woman, Sojourner Truth often was the focus of intense hostility. At a New York City speech on September 8, 1853, for example, some people had paid a twenty-five-cent admission just to have the chance to heckle the women speakers.[16] When Truth appeared, they became even more rowdy. To these closed-minded men, she represented "the two most hated elements of humanity. She was black and she was a woman."[17]

Truth tried publicly not to show discouragement. She kept on speaking out at all costs. At one meeting, a man questioned the validity of her work. He asked: "Old woman, do you think that your talk about slavery does any good? Do you suppose people care what you say? Why, I don't care any more for your talk than I do for the bite of a flea." Undaunted, Truth quickly replied, "Perhaps not, but, the Lord willing, I'll keep you scratching."[18]

Much of the power of Truth's talks were based on her unique experience as a former slave and a woman. As a result, it wasn't out of the ordinary for detractors to try to attack those very identities. In one now infamous 1858 incident in Indiana, a local doctor insisted that Truth was actually a man impersonating a woman. He claimed her voice was too manly to be a woman's. In an effort to embarrass her, he demanded she step outside with other women and take off her clothes to prove she was indeed what she said. As usual, Truth would not be deterred. Rather than agree to the request, she unbuttoned her blouse on the spot. She told the surprised crowd that baring her breast was not to her shame, but to theirs. Truth turned the doctor's argument to her own advantage by reminding the audience that she was proud to be a black woman.

CHAPTER SIX

TRAVELING TO WASHINGTON

By the late 1850s, tension was brewing between the North and the South. The Southern states were growing increasingly fearful that the Northern states were trying to end slavery, and in so doing, take over most of the political power in the nation. The North, on the other hand, feared that the Southern states were trying to spread slavery to new western territories in order to win more political power for themselves. While Truth was obviously interested in these debates, she never actively engaged in the politics concerning them. In fact, around 1857 it looked as if Truth were semi-retired.

During her travels, Truth had visited Battle Creek, Michigan, a city that was known for its progressive attitudes and racial tolerance. In 1857, Truth decided to sell her house in Northampton and move to Michigan. At first, she lived in Harmonia, a community six miles from Battle Creek. Truth's daughters, Diana and Elizabeth, and their two sons, Samuel Banks and James Caldwell, went with her to Harmonia. Of all her grandchildren, Truth was particularly close to Sammy. He became her traveling companion and accompanied her on almost all her adventures and speaking tours.

By 1860, Truth sold the house in Harmonia to her daughter Sophia in order to move to Battle Creek. In Battle Creek, Truth's daughters hoped their mother would relax a bit. Perhaps for a short time she did. However, with the country becoming more divided over issues such as slavery and states' rights, it was inevitable that Truth would not be able to sit still for long.

THE FIGHT OVER SLAVERY

The same year Truth moved to Michigan, the United States Supreme Court ruled on the infamous *Dred Scott* case. Dred Scott was a Missouri slave who had moved with his master to the free state of Illinois and the free territory of Minnesota. Because he had lived on free soil, Scott decided to sue his master for his freedom. The case went all the way to the Supreme Court. In the end, the Supreme Court decided that Scott did not have the right to sue, since he was not a United States citizen. According to the Court, no black person could be a citizen. The ruling was a blow to the abolition movement. It meant that black Americans, even those who were free like Truth, were ineligible for United States citizenship and its privileges.

NOW READY:

THE

Dred Scott Decision.

OPINION OF CHIEF-JUSTICE ROGER B. TANEY,

WITH AN INTRODUCTION,

BY DR. J. H. VAN EVRIE.

ALSO,

AN APPENDIX,

BY SAM. A. CARTWRIGHT, M.D., of New Orleans,

ENTITLED,

"Natural History of the Prognathous Race of Mankind."

ORIGINALLY WRITTEN FOR THE NEW YORK DAY-BOOK.

THE GREAT WANT OF A BRIEF PAMPHLET, containing the famous decision of Chief-Justice Taney, in the celebrated Dred Scott Case, has induced the Publishers of the DAY-BOOK to present this edition to the public. It contains a Historical Introduction by Dr. Van Evrie, author of "Negroes and Negro Slavery," and an Appendix by Dr. Cartwright, of New Orleans, in which the physical differences between the negro and the white races are forcibly presented. As a whole, this pamphlet gives the *historical*, *legal*, and *physical* aspects of the "Slavery" Question in a concise compass, and should be circulated by thousands before the next presidential election. All who desire to answer the arguments of the abolitionists should read it. In order to place it before the masses, and induce Democratic Clubs, Democratic Town Committees, and all interested in the cause, to order it for distribution, it has been put down at the following low rates, for which it will be sent, free of postage, to any part of the United States. Dealers supplied at the same rate.

Single Copies	$0 25
Five Copies	1 00
Twelve Copies	2 00
Fifty Copies	7 00
One Hundred Copies	12 00
Every additional Hundred	10 00

Address

VAN EVRIE, HORTON, & CO.,

Publishers of DAY-BOOK,

No. 40 Ann Street, New York.

In the 1857 landmark case *Dred Scott v. Sandford*, the Supreme Court decided that no African American had the right to sue in federal court because African Americans were not American citizens.

Tensions over slavery sometimes led to violence. Throughout much of the nineteenth century, there were many slave uprisings in which groups of slaves violently rebelled against their white masters in hopes of winning their freedom. One of the worst incidents, however, was led not by a slave but by a militant white abolitionist named John Brown.

Although John Brown had long been outspoken and well-known for his stance on slavery, he became most famous for leading a violent raid in Virginia in 1859. Brown planned to free slaves through force, then train them as soldiers to attack slaveholders and free other slaves. In October 1859, he organized an attack on a military arsenal at Harpers Ferry, Virginia (now West Virginia). He planned to use the weapons he would steal to free more slaves. Brown's plans failed, however, when United States Marines put down the rebellion. Brown was tried, found guilty of treason, and on December 2, 1859, he was hanged. Many abolitionists in the North considered Brown a hero for his attack against slavery. Southerners, on the other hand, feared further attacks and took steps to increase their military preparations in case of another slave revolt—or a war.

CIVIL WAR LOOMING

More fuel was added to the fire in 1860, with the upcoming presidential election. Truth particularly liked one of the candidates because of his stance against the spread of slavery. His name was Abraham Lincoln.

As a Republican political leader, Lincoln did not aggressively work to outlaw slavery, but he did fight to confine it to states where it already existed. In 1854, Lincoln had spoken out against Senator Stephen Douglas's proposal—the famous Kansas-Nebraska bill. The bill gave citizens who lived in these newly created territories the right to vote whether they wanted to be admitted to the Union as a free state or a slave state. Despite criticism from politicians such as Lincoln, the bill passed in May 1854, but it caused many more problems than it solved.

Proslavery forces from Missouri crossed the border into the Kansas territory in order to try to swing the vote. Most of the citizens of Kansas, however, wanted to be admitted as a free state. When the supporters of slavery won the vote, the antislavery residents refused to acknowledge it or the new state government. The incident led to violence with attacks and counterattacks from both sides.

While abolitionists were somewhat mixed about their opinions of Lincoln, Southerners were dead set in theirs. They disliked his politics so much that they promised to secede—leave the Union—if he were elected president. In 1860, Lincoln won the election without a single Southern vote.

To a large degree, Lincoln, the Republican candidate, won the election because the Democratic party split, nominating two candidates. They were Stephen Douglas for the Northern Democrats and John Breckinridge for the Southern Democrats. The South stayed true to its word: Seven states of the Deep South seceded before Lincoln took office in March 1861 and formed the Confederate States of America. The country clearly seemed destined for civil war.

THE WAR BETWEEN THE STATES

As of April 12, 1861, there was no longer any doubt. Confederate troops attacked Fort Sumter, in Charleston, South Carolina, and the Civil War officially began. Although Truth still did not advocate violence, she gave her full support to the Union once war was declared.

In 1862, an old abolitionist friend named Josephine Griffing came to visit Truth in Michigan. Griffing invited Truth to join a new lecture tour. Truth immediately agreed and once again began traveling and speaking out against slavery just as passionately as ever. On one occasion, Griffing remembered Truth angrily telling a hostile crowd, "It seems that it takes *my* black face to bring out *your* black hearts; so it's well I came."[1] As usual, Truth wanted to make it clear that slavery and those who supported it were morally wrong.

Finally, on January 1, 1863, it looked as if the abolition movement had made progress. President Lincoln signed the Emancipation Proclamation, freeing slaves in the Confederate states. It said: "All persons held as slaves within any State or designated part of a State, the people whereof shall … be in rebellion against the United States, shall be then, thenceforward, and forever free."[2]

This was a major step for one of Truth's causes. However, the fight was far from over, especially since the country was in the middle of a war. Furthermore, the declaration by no means guaranteed black Americans equal rights. In fact, black men had not even been allowed to join the Union Army, despite the fact that many wanted to take

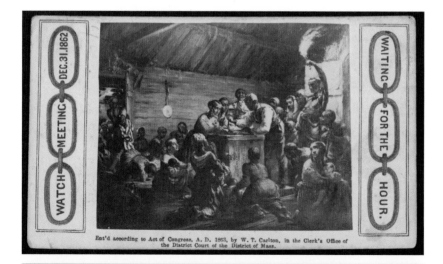

Ent'd according to Act of Congress, A. D. 1863, by W. T. Carlton, in the Clerk's Office of the District Court of the District of Mass.

This carte de visite shows African American men, women, and children gathered around a man with a watch, waiting for the Emancipation Proclamation.

an active part in the fight for their freedom. Along with other black leaders, most notably Frederick Douglass, Truth campaigned for the Union Army to accept black troops. By 1863, President Lincoln yielded to the abolitionist demand, and by April, the first black regiment, the Massachusetts 54th, was formed. Soon black men from across the Union were volunteering to serve. Among those brave men were Truth's grandson James Caldwell and two of Frederick Douglass's sons.

As her grandson fought on the front lines, Truth fought from behind them. She went door to door, collecting food for local troops. In one famous anecdote, a man refused to donate to Truth's food drive. She asked him his name and he replied, "I am the only son of my mother." Truth quickly retorted, "I am glad there are no more," and continued to the next house.[3]

Truth also composed songs to boost troops' morale. Her most famous was "The Valiant Soldiers," sung to the tune of the "Battle Hymn of the Republic." In the last verse, Truth told the story of Lincoln's allowing black soldiers to fight:

> *Father Abraham has spoken, and the message has been sent;*
> *The prison doors have opened, and out the prisoners went*
> *To join the sable army of African descent,*
> *As we go marching on—*[4]

The 54th Massachusetts Volunteer Infantry was the first African-American regiment in the US Army. The regiment's valiant fight at Fort Wagner on July 18, 1863, encouraged the enlistment of more African American soldiers.

A VISIT WITH THE PRESIDENT

Truth was thrilled with the progress the abolition-ists were making. She decided that she would go to Washington, D.C., and tell the president himself how pleased she was with his work. She made her way to Washington, D.C., with her grandson Sammy, visiting friends and lecturing along the way. Truth never doubted that Lincoln would meet with her.

"I shall surely go," she said. "I never determined to do anything and failed."[5]

As usual, Truth succeeded in doing what she put her mind to. On October 29, 1864, she met President Abraham Lincoln. Truth conveyed the story in a letter to a friend, which was then published in a later volume of her *Narrative*. Truth told Lincoln he was "the best president who has ever taken the seat."[6] Lincoln was flattered, but said there were others, particularly George Washington, who were much better presidents than he. Before leaving, Truth made certain to ask the president to sign her *Book of Life*. He wrote: "For Aunty Sojourner Truth, Oct. 29, 1864. A. Lincoln." Truth was very proud to have his autograph. As she left, she thought to herself, "I felt that I was in the presence of a friend, and I now thank God from the bottom of my heart that I always have advocated his cause."[7]

During this time, Washington, D.C. was not a very nice place to live, particularly for the poor and uneducated. After emancipation, many former slaves from Maryland and Virginia fled to the nation's capital in hopes of starting a new life. Unfortunately, although they were free, it was clear that black Americans' problems were not miraculously solved with their emancipation. With no money and little education or skills, it was difficult to support themselves. Many of these former slaves had to live in overcrowded and unsanitary areas of the city.

THE BUREAU OF REFUGEES, FREEDMEN, AND ABANDONED LANDS

In order to help, abolitionists created relief organizations to help black Americans make the transition from slavery to freedom. Toward the end of the war, the federal government began funding similar relief efforts by creating the Bureau of Refugees, Freedmen, and Abandoned Lands.[8] Known as the Freedmen's Bureau, the agency was set up to protect the rights of newly freed slaves, to temporarily provide them with food and shelter, to educate them, and to teach them a trade so they could find work.

Truth worked in both the abolitionists' and the federally funded organizations from 1864 to 1868. Her assignment for the Freedmen's Bureau was as a counselor at Freedmen's Village, located at Arlington Heights, Virginia—the former estate of Confederate General Robert E. Lee. At the village, Truth taught women domestic tasks such as cooking and sewing. She was a stickler when it came to cleaning. She always insisted that the residents at the village be neat and clean. Truth could often be heard chiding, "Be clean! be clean! for cleanliness is godliness."[9]

While still working for the Freedmen's Bureau, Truth heard the wonderful news that the war was over. On April 9, 1865, Confederate General

Sojourner Truth met President Abraham Lincoln on October 29, 1864. The president showed Truth a Bible that had been presented to him by appreciative Baltimore African Americans.

Robert E. Lee was surrounded at Appomattox Court House, Virginia. He surrendered to Union General Ulysses S. Grant, which marked the approaching end of the Civil War.

The good tidings did not last long, however. Five days later, on April 14, President Lincoln was shot by an actor and Confederate sympathizer named John Wilkes Booth while watching a play at Ford's Theatre in Washington, D.C. Lincoln died the next day. After Lincoln's death, Vice President Andrew Johnson succeeded him.

PUTTING THE COUNTRY BACK TOGETHER

Truth encouraged the freedmen not to lose hope. It was hard to keep morale up, though, especially since blacks still had no say in lawmaking processes. All that changed during Reconstruction, the period after the Civil War during which the Southern states were brought back into the Union. In 1865, the Thirteenth Amendment to the Constitution officially abolished slavery throughout the United States. It was not until 1870, after the Fifteenth Amendment to the United States Constitution was ratified, that the status of the freedmen finally changed. The amendment declared: "The right of citizens of the United States to vote shall not be denied or abridged by the United States or by any State on account of race, color, or previous condition of servitude." In theory, black citizens now had the same rights as white citizens, which meant they could vote and run for public office.

The news was only half good, though. While it granted black men the right to vote, women of all colors were still excluded. Many women's rights activists who had worked for abolition felt betrayed. On hearing the news that only men had won the right to vote, Truth said:

> There is a great stir about colored men getting their rights, but not a word about the colored women; and if colored men get their rights, and not colored women theirs, you see the colored men will be masters over the women, and it will be just as bad as it was before.[10]

Unfortunately, Truth and many of her fellow women's rights activists would not live to see the day that women's suffrage was won. The Nineteenth Amendment granting women the right to vote would not be ratified until 1920.

As a black woman, Truth had to deal with problems of her own in Washington, D.C. In order to get from place to place in the city, Truth often took streetcars. Although there was a law banning segregation—the practice of separating people by race—on the cars, some white passengers tried to

WOMEN'S SUFFRAGE

Women's rights activists were particularly disappointed in the fact that women were excluded from the guaranteed rights of the Fourteenth and Fifteenth amendments. They had been working for years to prevent just such an outcome. In an 1866 letter to Truth, famous suffrage leader Susan B. Anthony wrote:

Do you know that there are three men . . . who have dared to propose to amend the United States Constitution by inserting the word "male," thus shutting all women out by constitution from voting. . . . It is a most atrocious proposition, and I know Sojourner Truth will say, No, to it. God bless you, and help you to do the good work before you.[11]

give Truth a hard time for wanting to ride. Truth was very aware that she had the same right as everyone else in the city to ride the cars and would not let anyone tell her differently.

On one occasion, Truth signaled for several cars to stop, but none did. At the top of her voice, she yelled, "I want to ride! *I want to ride!! I WANT*

TO RIDE!!!"[12] Everyone was so surprised to see an elderly black woman screaming on the street corner, that not only did the streetcar stop, but all the traffic and passersby did, as well. Truth quickly stepped on the streetcar, much to the dismay of the conductor, who had tried to pass her. Several of the passengers laughed at the way Truth had triumphed over the conductor.

Another time, Truth was traveling with her friend Laura Haviland, a wealthy white woman. As the streetcar stopped in front of the two women, Truth

SOJOURNER TRUTH AND ROSA PARKS

Sojourner Truth's refusal to be ignored by public transportation officials is in many ways a precursor to an even more well-known civil rights institute. Nearly ninety years later Rosa Parks famously refused to give up her seat on a public bus to a white customer in 1955. Her actions led to a year-long boycott of the Montgomery buses and are considered a pivotal moment in the 20th Century U.S. Civil Rights Movement.

stepped forward to get on first. The conductor was very angry and pushed Truth out of the way, telling her to let the lady on first. Truth replied, "I am a lady too," and again tried get on. The conductor did not stop there. He grabbed Truth by the shoulder and violently tried to shove her out the door. Haviland told him to let her friend go at once, but he would not listen. He asked the white woman if Truth belonged to her. Angrily, she replied, "No, ... She belongs to humanity." The conductor once again shoved Truth against the door, this time so hard that he dislocated her shoulder.[13] The two women got off the car, but their fight certainly was not over. They wrote down the number of the car and reported the offense the next day. Truth had the conductor arrested on charges of assault and battery. Eventually, he lost his job because of the way he had treated Truth and her friend. Despite the fact that she was in her late sixties, Truth was still fighting for her rights and her beliefs with the same energy she had as a young woman.

CHAPTER SEVEN

MORE WORK TO DO

The Freedmen's Bureau worked tirelessly on behalf of African Americans, but actual progress was slow at best. No matter how much training was offered, there were simply too many former slaves and not enough jobs to go around. Racial tensions remained very high after the Civil War, so asking the federal government for more funding was always an uphill battle. For every person who argued that the Freedmen's Bureau needed more money, there was always someone else to insist it was not the government's job to help black Americans.

Watching poor, often homeless, free blacks living in the street without food or money, reminded Truth of the reason she had left New York City so many years before. She could not bear Washington any longer and felt it was time to move on. But before leaving, Truth decided that, if no one would find a solution to the problems that plagued the freed slaves, she would have to try and find one herself.

This 1866 poster attacking the Freedmen's Bureau depicts a racist caricature of an African American man, supported by government aid, lazing about at the expense of hardworking white men.

WORKING FOR LAND GRANTS

As Truth's position at the Freedmen's Village ended and she prepared to leave the city, she tried to think of possible ways to help improve living conditions. At first, Truth found jobs and homes up north for some of the freedmen she had come to know. In her *Narrative*, Truth claimed she made three trips from Rochester, New York, to a town two hundred miles south of Richmond, Virginia, in order to connect young men with positions she had found.[1] After a short while, though, Truth was no longer certain that this was the best plan of action. Since she could only find jobs for strong, young men, the women, children, and elderly were still left in poverty to fend for themselves.

Truth continued to watch conditions worsen despite her efforts. Soon, though, she thought of a new and better way to help. Truth believed that the United States government should set aside uninhabited land in the West to give the newly freed blacks, in the same way that reservations had been set aside for American Indians. Truth felt that her plan to obtain land grants would improve the miserable conditions in which free blacks lived. Truth also believed that allotting uninhabited land was the least the government could do for black Americans, considering all they had been through. "Our nerves and sinews, our tears and blood, have been sacrificed on the altar of this nation's avarice [greed]. Our unpaid labor has been a stepping-stone to its financial success. Some of its dividends must surely be ours," proclaimed Truth.[2] If African Americans were given land to cultivate on their own, they would surely be more independent and resourceful than they would if left homeless and uneducated in the squalor of big cities.

Truth's task was doubly hard. Not only did she have to convince freed blacks to relocate, but she had to convince the government to allot the land as well. Just as she had done in her abolitionist days, Truth tackled the problem by speaking out publicly. Much of her argument was based on an appeal to rich white men's pockets. Truth contended that too many black men lived off the government, thereby costing a lot in taxes. If freedmen were given their own land, they would have a greater incentive to support themselves, making them more productive members of society.[3]

A Boston newspaper reported on an 1871 speech Truth gave on the eighth anniversary of the Emancipation Proclamation, where she argued that the United States should give freed slaves land and "move them on it." "[G]et de ole pepul out," she said, "and build dem homes in de West where dey can feed themselves, and dey would soon be abel to be a pepul among you. Dat is my commission."[4]

Truth was also very concerned with educating African Americans in their potential new homes. She understood firsthand the difficulties of not being able to read and write. Therefore, she advocated education as a means of liberation.

As usual, Truth did not stop with lecturing. She believed the most direct way to get the government to listen to her was to speak to the government itself. So, she drafted a petition to Congress:

To the Senate and House of Representatives, in Congress assembled:—

Whereas, From the faithful and earnest representations of Sojourner Truth (who has personally investigated the matter), we believe that the freed colored people in and about Washington, dependent upon government for support, would be greatly benefited and might become useful citizens by being placed in a position to support themselves: We, the undersigned, therefore earnestly request your honorable body to set apart for them a portion of the public land in the West, and erect buildings thereon for the aged and infirm, and otherwise legislate so as to secure the desired results.[5]

Truth felt that the land grant project would be the culmination of her life work. Even though she was over seventy years old, she continued touring and speaking in order to win support for her proposal and signatures for her petition. She hoped to get enough signatures to "send tons of paper down to Washington."[6] Before she left to tour, Truth's friend Frances Titus offered to update her *Narrative*. The new version was published in 1875. It included news clippings, letters, and autographs from her *Book of Life*. As with the original version, Truth brought copies of her updated *Narrative* to sell at the meetings at which she spoke.

Although many people were willing to sign her petition, Truth was unable to find a senator willing

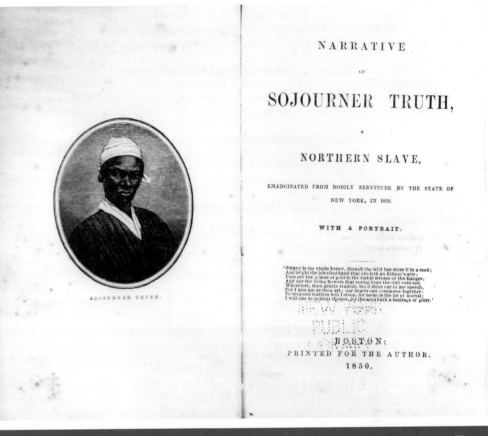

NARRATIVE

OF

SOJOURNER TRUTH,

A

NORTHERN SLAVE,

EMANCIPATED FROM BODILY SERVITUDE BY THE STATE OF

NEW YORK, IN 1828.

WITH A PORTRAIT.

'Sweet is the virgin honey, though the wild bee store it in a reed;
And bright the jewelled band that circleth an Ethiop's arm;
Pure are the grains of gold in the turbid stream of the Ganges;
And fair the living flowers that spring from the dull cold sod.
Wherefore, thou gentle student, bend thine ear to my speech,
For I also am as thou art; our hearts can commune together;
To meanest matters will I stoop, for mean is the lot of mortal;
I will rise to noblest themes, for the soul hath a heritage of glory.'

BOSTON:

PRINTED FOR THE AUTHOR.

1850.

SOJOURNER TRUTH.

In 1850, William Lloyd Garrison published Truth's memoirs under the title *The Narrative of Sojourner Truth: A Northern Slave*. As Truth never learned to read or write, she dictated the book's material to a friend.

to present it in Congress. Without any powerful political allies, she could not push her land grant mission any further.

In early 1875, Truth received some more bad news that put an end to her land grant project for the time. Her beloved grandson and companion, Sammy, was very ill. Truth rushed back to her home in Battle Creek to be with him. While she made it back in time to see him, he did not live much longer. He died in February 1875 at the age of twenty-four.

The time immediately following Sammy's death was very hard for Truth. Aside from his death, the Freedmen's Bureau had been cut off from federal funding. Truth had yet to find someone to present her petition to Congress, and it looked like she never would. As the years passed, it seemed that the government was becoming less concerned with the people it had helped to free.

FINAL EDITION OF THE NARRATIVE

The 1875 edition of *The Narrative of Sojourner Truth* that Frances Titus edited remains the final and most definitive of Truth's publication. But another version almost came out a few years later. An editor of the well-known antislavery and feminist publication New York *Independent* approached Truth in 1872. Theodore Tilton tried to convince Truth to let him tell her life's story. In her typical no nonsense style, Truth declined. Even though she was into her seventies she said she "expected to live a long time yet, and was going to accomplish 'lots' before she died, and didn't want to be 'written up' at present.[7]

WESTWARD MIGRATION

Then, in 1879, something astonishing happened. Tens of thousands of poor black freedmen began fleeing Southern states such as Mississippi and Louisiana and relocating to Kansas of their own accord.[8] Kansas was still a relatively unpopulated state, so it offered freedmen a chance to start a new life.

Since the government was doing very little to protect or help them, African Americans were afraid that life in the South would revert to the way it had been before the war. While African Americans were legally granted the same rights as whites, many white Southerners refused to accept the law. Segregation laws, known as Jim Crow laws, were passed by whites to separate the races. Some radically racist groups, such as the Ku Klux Klan, resorted to violence and even murder to keep blacks from achieving equal rights. Fearful that their hard won independence

This 1874 political cartoon illustrates the irony that slavery was replaced by two equally evil forces: the White League and the Ku Klux Klan.

IN
MEMORIAM
SOJOURNER
TRUTH
BORN A SLAVE IN
ULSTER Co. N.Y.
IN THE 18 TH
CENTURY
DIED IN
BATTLE CREEK
MICH.
NOV. 26, 1883
AGED ABOUT
105 YEARS
"IS GOD DEAD"
S.T.

Sojourner Truth died at her home in Battle Creek, Michigan, on November 26, 1883. She is buried at Oak Hill Cemetery, beside her beloved family.

was in danger, some black families thought it better to relocate.

Although it was not exactly the plan she had envisioned, Truth was thrilled that freedmen were taking their future into their own hands. Relief organizations similar to those set up in Washington, D.C., after the war were established to help the migrants get settled. For a time, Truth volunteered at the newly formed Kansas Freedmen's Relief Association along with her old friends Frances Titus and Laura Haviland.

By 1879, the migration had tapered off, and Truth, now in her eighties, was exhausted. She moved back to Battle Creek in January 1880. There, she lived with her daughters and their children.

By 1883, Sojourner Truth had fallen seriously ill. She died on November 26. Her funeral was one of the biggest Battle Creek had ever seen. Many of her famous colleagues, including Frederick Douglass, William Lloyd Garrison, and Elizabeth Cady Stanton, eulogized her.[9] Even at the end, Truth's legend was larger than life.

CHAPTER EIGHT

A LEGACY THAT LIVES ON

At a time when nearly every human right was denied Sojourner Truth, she still rose to become a nationally recognized advocate for justice and equality between races and sexes. Determined and aggressive, Truth let neither keep her from pursuing her goals. As an abolitionist, she worked tirelessly alongside some of the most famous antislavery voices of the day. For her work as a women's rights activist, Truth was remembered by Elizabeth Cady Stanton as "the most wonderful woman the colored race has ever produced."[1]

But perhaps Truth did not want to be remembered as just a woman *or* as just a black person. She took pride in being a *black woman* and fought hard to remind people of that very fact. Truth forced mostly male abolitionists to recognize that female slaves needed freedom as much as male slaves did, while pointing out to predominantly white women's rights activists that women of color should be included in their cause as well.

In 2009, Nancy Pelosi, Michelle Obama, and Hillary Clinton unveiled a bust of abolitionist Sojourner Truth in Emancipation Hall of the US Capitol.

Over one hundred years after her death, Sojourner Truth remains one of the most powerful symbols and examples of American black feminism. Statues in her honor were erected in Battle Creek, Michigan in 1999 and in Northampton, Massachusetts in 2002. In 2009, First Lady Michelle Obama, Hillary Clinton and then-Speaker of the House Nancy Pelosi looked on as Sojourner Truth became the first African American woman to be memorialized with a bust in the U.S. Capitol. During the unveiling of the statue, Mrs. Obama's comments highlighted Truth's prevailing importance and influence.

And just as Susan B. Anthony, Elizabeth Cady Stanton, Lucretia Mott would be pleased to know that we have a woman serving as the Speaker of the House of Representatives, I hope that Sojourner Truth would be proud to see me, a descendant of slaves, serving as the First Lady of the United States of America. And just as many young boys and girls have walked through this Capitol . . . . now many young boys and girls, like my own daughters, will come to Emancipation Hall and see the face of a woman who looks like them. All the visitors in the U.S. Capitol will hear the story of brave women who endured the greatest of humanity's indignities. They'll hear the story of Sojourner Truth, who didn't allow those indignities to destroy her spirit, who fought for her own freedom and then used her powers to help others; who fought for the right to vote and for the rights of all women.[2]

There is, of course, still work to be done. African Americans have struggled for full equality from Truth's time, through the civil rights movement of the 1950s and 1960s, and even to the present day. Likewise, although American women were granted the right to vote in 1920, they have fought throughout the twentieth century to win many of the same rights as men. In many parts of the world women and girls are still denied basic human rights. In 2014, the Nobel Peace Prize was awarded to 17-year old Pakistani girl Malala Yousafzai. Her work focused on the same types of equal rights and educational opportunities Truth advocated in 19th century America. It is in people's shared belief in the equality of all people that the legacy of Sojourner Truth lives on. Her strong belief in God, her family, herself, and the causes for which she continually fought have earned her a much deserved place in the history of American social reform.

CHAPTER NOTES

INTRODUCTION. SOJOURNER TRUTH AND NINETEENTH CENTURY SOCIAL REFORM

1. Ann D. Gordon, ed., Selected Papers of Elizabeth Cady Stanton and Susan B. Anthony, vol. 1. (New Brunswick, NJ: Rutgers University Press, 1997). (http://ecssba.rutgers.edu/docs/seneca.html).
2. Olive Gilbert, *The Narrative of Sojourner Truth,* ed. Henry Louis Gates (New York: Oxford University Press, 1991), pp. 131–135.
3. Andrea Atkin, "Sojourner Truth," *The Historical Encyclopedia of World Slavery*, ed. Junius P. Rodriguez (Santa Barbara, Calif.: ABC-CLIO, 1997), vol. 2, pp. 651–652.
4. Ibid.
5. Wendy Hamand Venet, *Neither Ballots Nor Bullets: Women Abolitionists and the Civil War* (Charlottesville: University Press of Virginia, 1991), p. 12.
6. Gilbert, pp. 131–132.
7. Ibid., p. 132.
8. Gilbert, p. 134.

CHAPTER 1. EARLY LIFE AS A SLAVE

1. Nell Irvin Painter, *Sojourner Truth: A Life, a*

Symbol (New York: W. W. Norton and Co., 1996), p. 12.

2. Olive Gilbert, *The Narrative of Sojourner Truth*, ed. Henry Louis Gates (New York: Oxford University Press, 1991), p. 17.
3. Nell Irvin Painter, *Sojourner Truth: A Life, a Symbol* (New York: W. W. Norton and Co., 1996), p. 7.
4. Gilbert, p. 17. Ibid., pp. 108–109.
5. Ibid., p. 16.
6. Ibid., p. 17.
7. Ibid., p. 26.
8. Ibid.
9. Ibid., p. 27.
10. Ibid., p. 28.
11. Ibid., pp. 24–25.
12. Painter, p. 14.
13. Gilbert, p. 33.
14. Painter, p. 15.
15. Gilbert, pp. 31–32.

CHAPTER 2. A FREE WOMAN

1. Margaret, Washington, *Sojourner Truth's America*. Urbana: University of Illinois Press, 2009, p. 56.
2. Olive Gilbert, *The Narrative of Sojourner Truth*, ed. Henry Louis Gates (New York: Oxford University Press, 1991), pp. 35–36.
3. Ibid., p. 38.

4. John Callow, "New York," *The Historical Encyclopedia of Slavery*, ed. Junius Rodriguez (Santa Barbara, Calif.: ABC-CLIO, 1997), vol. 2, p. 467.

5. Nell Irvin Painter, *Sojourner Truth: A Life, a Symbol* (New York: W. W. Norton and Co., 1996), p. 25.

6. Gilbert, p. 124.

7. Ibid., p. 43.

8. Ibid., p. 44.

9. Ibid., p. 45.

10. Ibid.

11. Ibid., pp. 69–72.

CHAPTER 3. A MOVE TO NEW YORK CITY

1. Nell Irvin Painter, *Sojourner Truth: A Life, a Symbol* (New York: W. W. Norton and Co., 1996), p. 38.

2. Olive Gilbert, *The Narrative of Sojourner Truth*, ed. Henry Louis Gates (New York: Oxford University Press, 1991), p. 71.

3. Ibid., p. 81.

4. Jacqueline Bernard, *Journey Toward Freedom: The Story of Sojourner Truth* (New York: W. W. Norton & Co., 1967), pp. 102–103.

5. Gilbert, p. 93.

6. Painter, p. 55.

7. Paul E. Johnson and Sean Wilentz, *The Kingdom of Matthias* (New York: Oxford

University Press, 1994), p. 97.

8. Ibid.

9. Bernard, p. 106.

10. Gilbert, p. 77.

11. Ibid., pp. 77–79.

12. Ibid., p. 103.

13. Ibid., p. 98.

14. Ibid., p. 100.

CHAPTER 4. JOINING THE ABOLITIONISTS

1. Olive Gilbert, *The Narrative of Sojourner Truth*, ed. Henry Louis Gates (New York: Oxford University Press, 1991), p. 114.

2. Ibid., p. 116.

3. Ibid., p. 117.

4. Erlene Stetson and Linda David, *Glorying in Tribulation: The Lifework of Sojourner Truth* (East Lansing: Michigan State University Press, 1994), p. 100.

5. Alive Eaton McBee, *From Utopia to Florence: The Story of a Transcendentalist Community in Northampton, Mass., 1830–1850* (Philadelphia: Porcupine Press, 1975), p. 22.

6. Elizabeth Frost-Knappman, *Women's' Suffrage in America, Updated Edition*, (New York: Facts on File, 2005), p. 59.

7. Jane H. Pease and William H. Pease, *The Fugitive Slave Law and Anthony Burns: A Problem in Law Enforcement* (Philadelphia:

Lippincott, 1975), pp. 11–12.

8. Frederick Douglass, *Narrative of the Life of Frederick Douglass, an American Slave*, ed. Houston A. Baker, Jr. (New York: Viking Penguin, 1986), pp. 77–87.

9. Quoted in McBee, pp. i–ii.

10. William L. Andrews, *To Tell a Free Story: The First Century of Afro-American Autobiography, 1760–1865* (Urbana: University of Illinois Press, 1986), pp. 97, 138.

11. Nell Irvin Painter, *Sojourner Truth: A Life, a Symbol* (New York: W. W. Norton and Co., 1996), p. 111.

CHAPTER 5. WOMEN'S RIGHTS ADVOCATE

1. Wendy Hamand Venet, *Neither Ballots Nor Bullets: Women Abolitionists and the Civil War* (Charlottesville: University Press of Virginia, 1991), p. 3.

2. Elisabeth Griffith, *In Her Own Right: The Life of Elizabeth Cady Stanton* (New York: Oxford University Press, 1984), p. xiv.

3. Constance Burnett, *Five for Freedom: Lucretia Mott, Elizabeth Cady Stanton, Lucy Stone, Susan B. Anthony, Carrie Chapman Catt* (New York: Greenwood Press, 1968), p. 31.

4. Olive Gilbert, *The Narrative of Sojourner Truth*, ed. Henry Louis Gates (New York: Oxford University Press, 1991), p. 318.

5. Miriam Gurko, *The Ladies of Seneca Falls: The Birth of the Woman's Rights Movement* (New York: Schocken Books, 1976), pp. 102–103.

6. Ibid.

7. Gurko, p. 165.

8. Nell Irvin Painter, *Sojourner Truth: A Life, a Symbol* (New York: W. W. Norton and Co., 1996), p. 143.

9. Ibid., p. 120.

10. Jacqueline Bernard, *Journey Toward Freedom: The Story of Sojourner Truth* (New York: W. W. Norton & Co., 1967), p. 171.

11. Gilbert, p. 168.

12. Nell Irvin Painter, *Sojourner Truth: A Life, a Symbol* (New York: W. W. Norton and Co., 1996), p. 139.

13. Quoted in Erlene Stetson and Linda David, *Glorying in Tribulation: The Lifework of Sojourner Truth* (East Lansing: Michigan State University Press, 1994), p. 132.

14. Joan D. Hedrick, *Harriet Beecher Stowe: A Life* (New York: Oxford University Press, 1994), p. 223.

15. Gilbert, pp. 151–153.

16. Stetson and David, p. 136.

17. Elizabeth Cady Stanton et al., eds., *History of Woman Suffrage* (New York: Fowler and Wells, 1881–1922), vol. 1, p. 567.

18. Gilbert, p. 312.

CHAPTER 6. TRAVELING TO WASHINGTON

1. Nell Irvin Painter, *Sojourner Truth: A Life, a Symbol* (New York: W. W. Norton and Co., 1996), p. 181.
2. John Hope Franklin, *The Emancipation Proclamation* (New York: Anchor Books, 1965), p. 91.
3. Painter, p. 182.
4. Olive Gilbert, *The Narrative of Sojourner Truth*, ed. Henry Louis Gates (New York: Oxford University Press, 1991), p. 126.
5. Ibid., p. 175.
6. Ibid., p. 178.
7. Ibid., p. 179.
8. Painter, p. 213.
9. Gilbert, p. 182.
10. Quoted in Patricia McKissack and Fredrick McKissack, *Sojourner Truth: Ain't I a Woman?* (New York: Scholastic Books, Inc., 1992), p. 154.
11. Gilbert, p. 28.
12. Ibid., p. 184.
13. Ibid., p. 282.

CHAPTER 7. MORE WORK TO DO

1. Olive Gilbert, *The Narrative of Sojourner Truth*, ed. Henry Louis Gates (New York: Oxford University Press, 1991), p. 191.

2. Ibid., p. 197.
3. Ibid., pp. 215–216.
4. Ibid., pp. 215–217.
5. Ibid., p. 199.
6. Ibid., p. 220.
7. Olive Gilbert, *The Narrative of Sojourner Truth*, ed. Henry Louis Gates (New York: Oxford University Press, 1991), pp. 234.
8. Nell Irvin Painter, *Sojourner Truth: A Life, a Symbol* (New York: W. W. Norton and Co., 1996), p. 243.
9. Ibid., pp. 254–255.

CHAPTER 8. A LEGACY THAT LIVES ON

1. Elizabeth Cady Stanton et al., eds., *History of Woman Suffrage* (New York: Fowler and Wells, 1881–1922) vol. 3, pp. 531–532.
2. "Remarks by the First Lady at the Sojourner Truth Bust Unveiling," The White House, Office of the First Lady (April 28, 2009. (https://www.whitehouse.gov/the-press-office/remarks-first-lady-sojourner-truth-bust-unveiling).

GLOSSARY

abolitionist—A person who worked to do away with slavery.

antebellum—years before the U.S. Civil War.

arsenal—A place where weapons are made and stored.

communal—As a group; in common.

Confederate States of America—The eleven states that withdrew from the United Sates in 1860 and 1861: Alabama, Arkansas, Florida, Georgia, Louisiana, Mississippi, North Carolina, South Carolina, Tennessee, Texas, and Virginia.

emancipation—the process of being set free.

enfranchisement—Being given the right to vote.

eulogize—To speak admiringly of someone after his or her death.

fanaticism—Extreme enthusiasm for a religion or other cause.

fraudulent—Deceptive.

Reconstruction—The process of restoring the former Confederate States to the Union after the Civil War. Lasting from 1865 to 1877, Reconstruction tried to reshape the conquered South through various efforts and to extend civil rights to the former slaves.

secede—To withdraw formally from a group or organization.

Sibyl—A mythological female prophet.

slander—Oral statements that hurt a person's reputation.

solidarity—a feeling or action of mutual support within a group.

suffrage—The right to vote.

Union—The states that remained loyal to the United States during the Civil War.

Yankee—A nickname for a Union soldier.

FURTHER READING

BOOKS

Day, Meredith, and Colleen Adams. *A Primary Source Investigation of Women's Suffrage.* New York, NY: Rosen Publishing, 2016.

Dudley Gold, Susan. *The Women's Rights Movement and Abolitionism.* New York, NY: Cavendish Square Publishing, 2016.

Freedman, Russell. *Abraham Lincoln and Frederick Douglass: The Story Behind an American Friendship.* Boston: Houghton Mifflin Harcourt, 2012.

Lusted, Marcia Amidon. *The Fight for Women's Suffrage.* Edina, MN: ABDO Publishing, 2012.

Morretta, Alison. *Frederick Douglass and William Garrison: A Partnership for Abolition.* New York, NY: Cavendish Square Publishing, 2016.

Morretta, Alison. *Legal Debates of the Antislavery Movement.* New York, NY: Cavendish Square Publishing, 2016.

Nardo, Don. *The Split History of the Women's Suffrage Movement: Suffragists' Perspective.* North Mankato, MN: Compass Point Books, 2014.

Turner, Ann. *My Name Is Truth: The Story of Sojourner Truth.* New York: Harper, 2015.

WEBSITES

Not For Ourselves Alone: The Story of Elizabeth Cady Stanton and Susan B. Anthony.
www.pbs.org/stantonanthony/movement
This PBS companion website features primary source
  documents, photographs, and commentary regard-
  ing the fight for the women's vote in America.

Rights for Women: The Suffrage Movement and Its Leaders. National Women's History Museum.
*www.nwhm.org/online-exhibits/rightsforwomen/index
.html*
This website tells the story of the abolition and wom-
  en's suffrage movements and provides ancillary
  resources such as a quiz, timeline, and a virtual
  tour.

Women's Rights National Historical Park at Seneca Falls
www.nps.gov/wori/index.htm
This site tells the story of the first Women's Rights
  Convention held in Seneca Falls, New York.

INDEX